THE PROFESSIONAL'S GUIDE TO
LONG-TERM INVESTING

www.amplifypublishinggroup.com

The Professional's Guide to Long-Term Investing: What to Buy, When to Sell, and the Factors Every Investment Manager Ought to Consider

For more information, please contact:
Amplify Publishing, an imprint of Amplify Publishing Group
620 Herndon Parkway, Suite 220
Herndon, VA 20170
info@amplifypublishing.com

Library of Congress Control Number: 2024911662

CPSIA Code: PRV0924A

ISBN-13: 979-8-89138-144-5

Printed in the United States

To my wife and daughters

CHARLES F. POHL

THE PROFESSIONAL'S GUIDE TO
LONG-TERM INVESTING

WHAT TO **BUY**, WHEN TO **SELL**,
AND THE FACTORS EVERY INVESTMENT
MANAGER OUGHT TO CONSIDER

amplify
an imprint of Amplify Publishing Group

CONTENTS

INTRODUCTION

I worked at Dodge & Cox for thirty-eight years. Mr. Cox used to say that they founded the firm in 1930 to look out for the interests of their investors. He felt there were numerous problems with investment advisors in the 1920s, and he could help launch an alternative.

In my time at the firm, we continued to always put the investor first. We didn't chase fads. We had one fund for US stocks, one for international stocks, a balanced fund, an income fund, a global bond fund, and an emerging markets fund. All the funds were introduced after much thought and consideration. I believe that a big part of our long-term success was due to the small number of funds we had. Many of the largest firms have fifty to three hundred funds, or even more. We never closed a US fund. Many other firms launch funds and then close the ones that don't work out. Some firms have more funds that they've closed than they still have open. I think the way we chose to do things has led to our long-term success over the years.

It has been demonstrated (as seen in the chart on the next page) that we have one of the best long-term track records of any large investment manager. At one point, I could have named every single security that we owned and told you something useful about it. How many other chairs of investment firms could make that claim? How many others can even name all their own funds?

This book is about long-term investing. It is about the elements that one needs to consider regarding an investment in order to become successful. I learned over time that there are no easy answers to achieving investment success. The world is always changing. But by understanding the fundamentals of business value and recognizing what successful investors need to pay attention to, you can uncover opportunities and avoid traps. There are many books about investing, but this one is different because it is meant not to help you capitalize on short-term trends but to show you what it means to be a long-term investor, how to properly evaluate companies, and how to make decisions that you can firmly stand behind.

Top 20 Fund Companies: Relationship Between Ratings, Expenses, and Assets
Asset-management firms continued their broad trend of lowering fees over the last year. Lower fees, which are taken directly out of performance, are beneficial for the end investor. Firms such as Vanguard, Dodge & Cox, and State Street have delivered impressive returns while charging among the lowest fees.

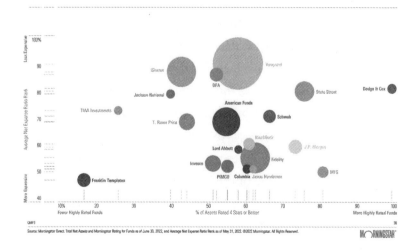

Source: Morningstar Direct. Total Net Assets and Morningstar Rating for Funds as of June 30, 2022, and Average Net Expense Ratio Rank as of May 31, 2022. ©2022 Morningstar. All Rights Reserved.

In the book, I cover the key areas that I paid attention to as a professional looking for the right investment opportunities: a company's accounting decisions, the nuts and bolts of the business itself (what I call "franchise"), the management and governance of a company, how the stock is valued, how to forecast going forward, when to sell, and how to think about risk. Taken together, I hope these tools empower you to be a more effective, more informed, and more successful long-term investor.

CHAPTER 1

UNDERSTANDING THE INVESTMENT LANDSCAPE

Before we dive into the topics that will make up the bulk of this book—helping investors understand how to evaluate individual companies and organizations as to their investment suitability—it is worth taking some time here at the start to understand the various participants in the securities markets, where you may fit, and how this book can help.

In the most basic sense, to make money in the securities markets with a return that outperforms a benchmark index, you must be better than other investors. Otherwise, you will lose. This is hard in an environment where there is a lot of knowledge and a lot of competition. There are a large number of retail investors and mutual funds who serve them. These funds and investors tend to invest in whatever has done well recently, whether that means particular sectors or individual investments. Mutual funds that invest in hot areas will be easier to sell. Retail investors tend to want to do today what they should have done yesterday. They end up following a rule that is the reverse of the conventional "buy low and sell high" wisdom. They buy after good performance and sell when things struggle. Buying high and selling low is a terrible way to make money over the long term.

Hedge funds make up another large segment of trading volume in today's marketplace. These funds have very high, asymmetric fees, typically 1 to 2 percent of the money under management along with 20 percent of the investment profits. Due to the high fees, clients have little patience for underperformance. As a result, hedge funds are under great pressure to do well. This requires them to engage in short-term strategies, guessing quarterly earnings or speculating on the news of the day. Generally, they are not long-term investors. They tend to have high turnover, which can be quite expensive over time due to transaction costs. They also need to take on significant risk. If the risks pay off, they are richly rewarded. If the risks result in losses, the hedge fund does not share in the losses—only the client loses money. Often, hedge funds have high-water marks, which means that they don't earn their performance fees until the client has made money. Hedge funds that fall too far below their high-water marks tend to close down.

Another type of investor is the activist investor. The most successful activist strategies involve getting a company to break itself up or sell itself outright. Some activists try to replace management or change corporate strategy. These approaches have tended to be less successful over time, although there are exceptions.

Over the past couple of decades, quantitative investors have grown in importance. These investors scour numeric databases looking for relationships between past data and future performance. Simple investment strategies, such as investing in low price-to-earnings or low price-to-book ratios, may have worked well in the past. But now, with organizations completely focused on quantitative data, companies with low ratios are picked over endlessly, and there are no obvious bargains to find. I expect these strategies to yield poor returns going forward compared to their historical results. The honest truth is that there are no simple strategies for consistently making money. If there were, everyone would pursue them, and they would cease to exist.

Index funds have become a larger and larger part of the market. Part of the reason for this is their low management fees and low transaction costs. The management fees can be very low because the fund does not actually do any research on the companies it is investing in. The funds merely buy all the securities in an index in proportion to their weights. A subindustry has grown up around index funds, second-guessing additions and deletions from the indexes and trying to game the index funds. As index funds become a larger and larger proportion of all money invested, there is the danger that security prices will become less representative of their underlying value. An index fund makes no pretense of trying to value a business. It counts on others to price the security accurately and take advantage of the public nature of transactions. However, as active managers become a smaller part of the market, this process breaks. If a larger and larger percentage of the market is simply automatic, security prices will be less and less accurate. This opens up opportunities for those who do the work.

My suspicion is that the opportunities for long-term active and informed investors right now are greater than they have been for many years. Hence the value of a book like this and the remainder of the discussions to come.

CHAPTER 2
ACCOUNTING

Accounting, at its core, is a system that helps us describe a business and, specifically, becomes key to establishing a valuation for the business. Yet while many people presume accounting numbers to be sacrosanct, this is not the case. Understanding accounting is critical to evaluating a company and whether the numbers it presents can be trusted.

The modern accounting system is actually much newer than many of us realize. For almost 150 years after the precursor to the New York Stock Exchange began in 1792, companies were not required to issue financial statements—which makes you wonder what people were basing their investment decisions on. Eventually, in the wake of the Great Depression, statements ended up being mandated by the SEC. The Securities Act of 1933—the "Truth in Securities Act"—required disclosure of material information regarding securities, and the Securities Act of 1934 established the SEC, prohibited insider trading, and required companies with more than $10 million in assets, whose securities are held by more than 500 owners, to file annual and other periodic reports. This was the first step in requiring companies to release standardized accounting statements.

The modern accounting principles that corporations are currently required to adhere to under the law involve a set of choices, both on the macro level, in terms of what we account for, and on the micro level, in terms of the choices each company makes in how it calculates its numbers.

Traditional versus Modern Businesses

From a big-picture perspective, most accounting principles were designed to describe traditional businesses, the kind that existed fifty or one hundred years ago when accounting principles were first standardized. In their excellent 2016 book, *The End of Accounting and the Path Forward for Investors and Managers*, authors Baruch Lev and Feng Gu explain how accounting principles were indeed designed for physical assets.[1]

Accounting, even as practiced today, is based largely on physical assets and concepts such as depreciation. This framework may be excellent for evaluating older, traditional businesses such as aluminum manufacturing, but current accounting principles fall quite short in describing more modern companies that are highly dependent on intellectual property and brand names. These valuable assets are not often accounted for appropriately, and these assets do not depreciate in the same way that a traditional machine or plant does. Thus, we must take the numbers with a grain of salt when looking specifically at modern businesses that function in ways that businesses didn't in the past.

Lev and Gu show that physical assets are, in fact, declining as a percentage of investment. Intangible assets, like research and development, brand names/incumbency, acquisition of customers/customer relationships, and the existence of a high-quality workforce, are all assets that may now take precedence over the physical. The overall effect of this may actually dwarf most of the other issues discussed in this chapter. In recent years, the percentage of variance explained by the book value of a company versus the stock price has plummeted due to the fact that the book value simply does not properly reflect these intangible assets. See the graph that follows, from Lev and Gu,[2] as an illustration of how much the percentage has fallen.

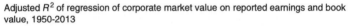

Adjusted R^2 of regression of corporate market value on reported earnings and book value, 1950-2013

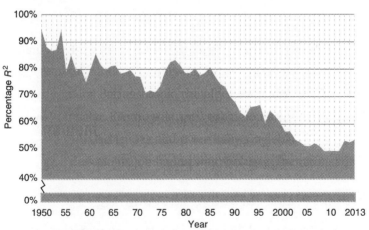

Share of Corporate Market Value Attributed to Earnings and Book Value

Lev and Gu's data also shows that the investment rate on intangible assets has been significantly higher in recent years than the investment rate on tangible assets.[3]

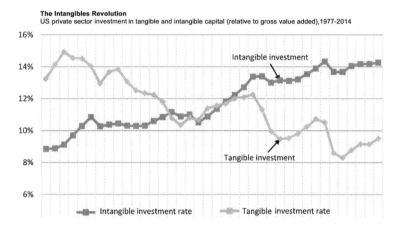

The Intangibles Revolution
US private sector investment in tangible and intangible capital (relative to gross value added),1977-2014

Intangible investment

Tangible investment

Intangible investment rate   Tangible investment rate

In their book, they provide a new methodology for calculating value, taking intangibles into account, and they show how that methodology can improve investment results. It is hard to argue that they are not on to something. I highly recommend their work if you are looking to explore this issue more deeply.

Fraud versus "Creative" Accounting

Accounting can end up being used as a way to mislead investors about the nature of a business. Two types of issues present themselves when examining a company's accounting statements, both of which I will discuss in this chapter. One is outright fraud.

The other is the creation of misleading financial statements. Misleading financial statements may be entirely legal. There is a certain amount of leeway allowed when generating financial statements, with some assumptions and tactics being more conservative and others less conservative, extending to tactics that deliberately confuse or mislead potential investors. More conservative accounting is often indicative of the culture or mentality of an organization. Liberal accounting treatments may indicate that management is always looking to cut corners. Misleading numbers—or, worse, outright fraud—in one part of an organization likely indicates a wider problem. At best, it is an indication of poor controls. At worst, it may be an indication of a management team or culture that is fundamentally corrupt.

Earnings versus Cash Flow: Accruals and Receivables

One of the primary ways a company will mislead involves choices made around the recognition of sales. We can often spot issues by noticing a difference between earnings and cash flow. One would think that a company's sales would be a fairly reliable number, easy to calculate and verify, but often that is not the case. We all understand the idea of buying things in a store and paying for them at the point of purchase. Even in a seemingly straightforward sale like this, there is the potential for accounting issues to arise. Is there a possibility to return the item after purchase? If so, has the seller appropriately reserved for potential returns? What about any warranties made regarding the sale? Is there sufficient reserve for any warranty costs? Was the sale made on the basis of credit? If so, is there adequate reserve for potential bad debts?

At MicroStrategy, a Virginia-based software company, customers were pushed to sign contracts right before the end of the quarter, and revenue was recognized on signing rather than on the actual receipt of income, or the services being performed.[4] Things had been going well for the company—too well, in fact. The company went public in 1998 with a valuation of more than $200 million. By early 2000, it was worth $13 billion, and *Forbes* magazine investigated why there had been such an increase so quickly.[5] It turned out that not only was revenue being recorded too early, but suspicious transactions were taking place, where money was flowing between buyers and sellers, allowing both sides to record revenue. For instance, the company signed a deal with electronics giant NCR, where MicroStrategy would purchase an $11 million warehouse and NCR's $14 million information analysis business, and, in return, NCR would buy $27.5 million of products and services from MicroStrategy.[6] Once the *Forbes* article went public, the accounting giant PricewaterhouseCoopers, which had recently signed off on MicroStrategy's financial reports, reconsidered and restated the numbers, and the company's share price plummeted by more than 90 percent.[7] An SEC investigation followed, with an accusation of fraud that was ultimately settled. More recently, in 2022, more accounting issues emerged at MicroStrategy, with the SEC disagreeing with how MicroStrategy treated its Bitcoin holdings[8] and cofounder and executive chairman Michael Saylor ending up accused of evading $25 million in Washington, DC, taxes.[9]

There is, of course, a difference between making fraudulent assumptions about revenue and merely unreasonable ones. Credit losses, in particular, change with the strength of the economy, so what looks like a reasonable assumption when times are good can change into a very flawed assumption when conditions evolve. Every economic cycle I've been through has involved the rise of consumer credit companies that take risks the established lenders won't . . . and it all ends badly when the economy shifts into recession. One example today is financial technology (fintech) companies extending credit with supposedly better technology, but the results likely won't be pretty. I remember back in the 1980s when Citibank had what they called a "fifteen-minute mortgage." It was highly automated and basically eliminated the underwriting process in the interest of speed. They thought they had quantified the risks, but they hadn't done it effectively, and it ended very badly once the cycle turned.

Even ignoring credit issues, and the possibility of returns, there is the question of whether a customer actually believes that a transaction has taken place at all. Accrual is an accounting term referring to when income or expenses are recorded, which may not be the same point at which payment for a sale is received or an expense is actually incurred. A company may record a sale based on what a customer regards as a trial period. In other words, a product may be shipped and be in use by the customer, but it has not been paid for, and may never be paid for depending on whether the customer decides to go ahead with the purchase. If these trials are recorded as earnings, it will be misleading to investors who may not realize that a significant percentage of these "earnings" will never convert into actual cash received.

Al Dunlap, who had earned a reputation as a cost-cutter and job-slasher—and the nickname "Chainsaw Al"—was hired as the CEO and chairman at Sunbeam Corporation in July 1996.[10] By early 1998, it appeared he had engineered an effective turnaround, at least until a Paine Webber analyst took a close look at the company's financials. There was an unusually large number of grills that had apparently been sold in the last quarter of 1997, an atypical season for people to buy grills. As it turned out, Dunlap had been using a bill-and-hold strategy, promising retailers big discounts if they would agree to purchase the grills now, with Sunbeam holding them in third-party warehouses and not shipping them until customers ordered.[11] This was not illegal, but it was misleading, to say the least, and the SEC investigated. Dunlap was fired, and Dunlap and other company executives eventually agreed to pay the SEC $500,000 to settle its charges and an additional $15 million to settle a class action lawsuit brought by shareholders.[12]

An example of fraud with a similar fact pattern is Sterling Homex in the early 1970s. The company was building manufactured housing and had started shipping it, but there were no end customers for the product. They dumped the product in empty fields but recorded these as sales because the product had, in fact, "shipped." The stock went through the roof temporarily . . . and then the company filed for bankruptcy because it had no cash flow. It recorded a tremendous amount of fictitious earnings because no one was actually buying the manufactured housing.

Even absent fraud, these kinds of issues are especially worth examining in companies where the sales force is highly incentivized to sell more product—in other words, when the sales force is compensated on a commission basis. Some sales commissions are levered in the sense that each incremental sales dollar carries with it a higher commission rate, a particularly common model for products with a high gross margin like software. With levered sales commissions, there is a powerful incentive to push product out the door before the quarter ends.

The tech company Oracle ran its commissions this way, and it eventually worked out well for them, but they experienced real problems in the 1980s. Banks commissioned an independent audit of Oracle's books because they were so concerned with what Oracle had been recording as revenue.

It's not necessarily just about sales commissions, but often about a company's larger incentives to get its quarterly earnings as high as possible. I followed the tech industry in the 1980s and saw this happen frequently. These companies have to show growth, so they will try to pump as much product out the door at the end of a quarter as possible. Everyone will be working overtime, doing whatever they can to close deals. But shipping product and getting paid for it are often two different things. Accounts receivable will balloon upward for companies doing this, so the discrepancy between actual cash flow and earnings grows. You book the earnings when you ship the product, but taking into account clients who return it, or who perhaps never even ordered it, the cash ultimately received will not be nearly as high as reported.

When to actually book a sale—if you're not trying to deliberately mislead—ends up being a judgment call, and judgment calls inevitably create opportunity for people who want to boost earnings. If you focus only on the reported earnings and don't look closely at cash flow as well, you could be missing most of the story.

Another example relevant here is Fruit of the Loom. The company had incredibly aggressive targets for the management team and a big payout for these key employees if they met those targets. The company ended up meeting the targets, but there were a number of accounting irregularities involved in doing so. Eventually, the irregularities came to light, and the stock collapsed. Fruit of the Loom filed for bankruptcy in 1999. (In 2002, Warren Buffett's Berkshire Hathaway bought Fruit of the Loom for approximately $800 million in cash.)

There is also the example of Computer Associates. The company had an unbelievably generous compensation plan based on achieving certain targets. They were, in fact, achieved, and the company's top executives received tremendous payouts—except that, as it turned out, the company didn't actually make the sales that it reported. Executives manipulated the numbers and ended up in prison for it. The CEO, Sanjay Kumar, inflated sales figures in order to earn a $330 million bonus in 1998. How did he do it? According to the *New York Times*, "The company rolled sales figures from new quarters into previous earnings figures, a practice employees called the 35-day month . . . [and later Kumar] approved a $3.7 million payment to silence a potential witness."[13]

From the SEC complaint: "During the period from at least Jan.

1, 1998, through Sept. 30, 2000, Computer Associates prematurely recognized over $3.3 billion in revenue from at least 363 software contracts that Computer Associates, its customer, or both parties, had not yet executed, in violation of GAAP . . . . Executives, including [defendant Kumar] . . . held Computer Associates' books open for several days after the end of each quarter to improperly record in that quarter revenue from contracts that were not executed by customers or Computer Associates until several days or more after the expiration of the quarter . . . [resulting in inflated revenue in each quarter of FY2000 of] approximately 25%, 53%, 46%, and 22%."[14]

The company also made the choice to recognize certain revenue as license payments, which would be recognized up front, boosting sales figures, rather than as maintenance, which would be recognized over time and reduce current sales. The reality was that the company's software was quite critical for its customers, and the business was fairly stable. The accounting shenanigans obscured this reality and created a very different picture.

Kumar wound up being sentenced to twelve years in prison.

Earnings versus Cash Flow: "Adjusted" Earnings

It is important to realize that "adjusted" earnings may not always be reflective of reality, even when a company claims they are. There are companies that choose, for example, to buy intellectual property rather than spending internally on research and development. They can then exclude the amortization of the IP assets in order to "adjust" their earnings, which can potentially overstate earnings in a significant way. These are judgment calls, but it is important to ask whether adjusted earnings are actually reflecting the state of the business or obscuring the reality of what is happening.[15]

Accounts Payable

Expansion of accounts payable is generally a good thing in that it generates cash. Contraction of accounts payable consumes cash. One should look deeper when the number is increasing or decreasing rapidly. It may be an indicator that the company is not paying its bills on time (a bad thing), or it may be an indicator that the company is holding onto its cash for as long as possible before paying those bills (a good thing). It may indicate more activity (a good thing), but it may just be a timing issue. You only know if you look more closely.

Inventory Tricks

The Cost of Goods Sold (COGS) is calculated as the value of the starting inventory, plus purchases, minus the ending inventory. If inventory increases during a particular period, this has the effect of reducing the cost of goods sold calculation to less than the value of the product that was, in fact, sold. This is because you still have to consider the changing value of the available inventory. The real earnings end up being worse than they look because you've absorbed some of those costs into the inventory. You're then left with more inventory than you had initially, and possibly a buildup of inventory that you may not be able to sell at all. This happens when companies have manufacturing lines to run, overmanufacture their products, and wind up with huge inventory that they end up having to mark down in order to move product. It is important to look deeper than the COGS number alone in order to actually figure out what the situation looks like. Is the company having to increase manufacturing (and inventory) because of pent-up demand, or have they manufactured too much, and will they have to discount in order to get rid of it?

We should also discuss LIFO (last in, first out) versus FIFO (first in, first out) inventory calculations. Where this becomes an issue is in periods of rapidly rising inflation, where a product produced a couple of years ago will have been made at a much lower cost than one produced today. In that situation, using LIFO is much more conservative than FIFO. On the other hand, in a situation where a product is quickly going obsolete, such as in the case of cell phones, FIFO may be more conservative because you want to make sure to account for the rapidly aging inventory.

These calculations can make a real difference in the financial statements, so they are important to pay attention to. One example to look at is Exxon Mobil, where the company used LIFO accounting in order to understate earnings and escape added criticism over the company's excessive profits. As the *Wall Street Journal* reported, "A string of record profits at Exxon Mobil Corp. has drawn howls from some politicians, but earnings at the world's largest oil company are, by at least one measure, understated."[16] LIFO is, in fact, banned under International Financial Reporting Standards for precisely this reason—that it may understate earnings.

Revenue/Loss Recognition: Rapid Growth in Credit

There are many cases where a company experiences rapid growth in credit, but losses are not recognized until some period of time later. While credit is growing rapidly, this delay can lead to an overstatement of earnings. This is a problem for banks especially, but not just banks. For example, credit card debt losses tend to peak eighteen months after credit is extended. If you're growing credit very rapidly, the losses will be a very small part of the credit extended at first, but if the rate of credit expansion ever slows, the losses will start to balloon. If the credit expansion goes negative—meaning you are recognizing losses to a greater extent than new credit is being extended—it can consume the whole enterprise and destroy it.

This is most dangerous in the case of long-term investment projects such as the construction of office buildings. A building may take five years to construct. A company won't discover whether the credit was good until the building is completed and it needs to start leasing it. For those first five years, the accountants will plug in an assumption about what the loss rate is going to be—but they don't actually know. This can create a real disconnect between the reported earnings and what turn out to be the actual earnings. In situations where the rental market softens during the time of construction, this can change the calculations dramatically as far as whether a project is worth embarking on in the first place.

There is someone building apartments in Manhattan right now thinking he can get a certain rent, but if the market softens by

20 percent, he will be in trouble. Deepwater oil drilling is another area where this issue shows up. Projects in this space can take ten years to complete, so companies that do deepwater drilling or make the supplies to enable the process can be very risky. For this industry specifically, the long time horizons combined with regulatory changes made investments extremely challenging at the end of the last century. In 1990, President George H. W. Bush placed a ten-year moratorium on all new offshore drilling, and in 1998, President Bill Clinton extended the moratorium until 2012.[17] It is hard to justify investments when you do not even know if the project you are investing in will ever be allowed to happen.

Rapid growth of credit in just about any industry context is a red flag, and it merits looking further into the assumptions of loss and how deferred the actual losses will be. Projects that have long time horizons are far more dangerous on this front than shorter-term projects, where any actual losses will make themselves known more quickly.

Depreciation

There are different rates of depreciation—and this can be used to manipulate earnings in ways that are not always apparent. As with everything else in this chapter, it is all about choices. I can build a manufacturing plant and depreciate it at different rates. Some of those choices may be justified, but others may be designed to make my financial statements look a certain way.

There are reasons for flexibility in the choice of how to depreciate. Suppose I have a semiconductor plant, and the equipment—which will be the bulk of the cost of the plant—will be obsolete in five years. I may want to depreciate it all within those five years. An ethylene plant may make more sense to depreciate over thirty years because the technology is not evolving as rapidly.

Because there is judgment involved, it is worth looking at companies in similar industries and what rates they are using for depreciation. If the company you are analyzing is doing things differently from its competitors, the question to ask is: *Why?* Is it depreciating assets slower or faster? If there is a slower rate of depreciation, costs will be lower, and earnings will appear higher. This is something to be aware of.

The example of Waste Management—"one of the most egregious accounting frauds . . . ever seen," according to the SEC—is relevant here.[18] Among the company's fraudulent practices was assigning inflated salvage values to garbage trucks, thus extending their life as far as the accounting went, and lowering the depreciation. Thus, income appeared significantly higher than it otherwise would have.[19] Waste Management's "accounting tricks," according to the *New York Times*, "allowed the company to hide about $1.7 billion in expenses from 1992 through part of 1997."[20]

Expensing of Stock Options

One specific area with potential for balance sheet manipulation is in the expensing of stock options to company management or other employees. Cash compensation is expensed, as are bonuses. Yet stock options do not always appear on the balance sheet, even though these stock options, particularly for some technology companies, can be quite large. These are often not expensed as part of management compensation, though the rules over time have varied. For a smart analyst, this issue can be dealt with fairly easily. The value of the stock options can be looked up in the proxy, and it is worth deducting the amount from the income statement in order to get a better understanding of the profitability of the company. Otherwise, you risk being misled.

Indeed, as the *New York Times* wrote two decades ago, "Options, which are not counted as an expense and thus inflate earnings, bring with them a powerful incentive to cheat. They hold out the promise of wealth beyond imagining. All it takes is a set of books good enough to send a stock price soaring, if only for a while. If real earnings are not there, they can be manufactured—for long enough, in any case, for executives to cash out."[21]

Reserves and the Smoothing of Earnings

The market tends to value smooth earnings streams much more highly than erratic ones. Given this, companies do a lot to try to smooth out their earnings, some of it legitimate and some less so.

Companies have particular flexibility in this area when it comes to establishing reserves for various possibilities. I've already mentioned reserves for returns, credit, and warranties, but there are more. Companies can and should establish reserves for lawsuits, though this is often a problem because companies feel that if they put a certain amount of money in reserve for ongoing lawsuits, they are basically informing plaintiffs' attorneys that this is the amount they expect a case to settle for. Thus, there is great reluctance to establish reserves for ongoing litigation, and this almost always leads to a problem in the end. The company certainly doesn't want to overreserve, and potentially send a signal to attorneys to ask for more, so they underreserve, if they even reserve anything at all.

More broadly, if a company is having a good quarter, they may feel an urge to create new reserves in order to depress earnings temporarily and then feed that money back in by reducing reserves in a weak quarter. Particularly smooth earnings, especially when compared with other companies in the same industry, are suspicious, and should raise a red flag that there is a lot of improper earnings management happening.

The first subprime mortgage company to collapse during the financial crisis, New Century Financial, tried to manage earnings by adjusting reserves—to disastrous effect. Rather than increase its allowance for loan losses as delinquencies increased, it lowered its allowance, feeding that money back into earnings and completely concealing the reality of the situation. Eventually, it had to announce a restatement of earnings, which sent its stock into a tailspin from which it never recovered; the SEC charged management with securities fraud.[22]

The reality is that reserves of all kinds are really just judgment calls. I remember talking to a CEO after a merger. I asked how he decided how big a reserve to take, and he said, "I told my guys to put down a number big enough to cover a potential disappointment." There was no real basis to the number.

It isn't just reserves that can help a company smooth earnings.

You can often accrue expenses in different periods, depending on when they will be most useful to your financial statement. Suppose you buy a bunch of staples for your staplers. There is an open question of how you will record that as a cost. You could record it when you buy them, amortize the cost over time, or say you didn't use any staples this period and wait to accrue the cost until the next period. Or perhaps the one after that. You need to look carefully to uncover some of these potential tricks.

General Electric is a good example here. As reported by financial journalist William Cohan and discussed in an article in *Business Insider*, "[CEO Jack Welch] made it his mission to beat Wall Street's forecasts, and deliver slow, steady growth that would secure a higher valuation for GE stock. He oversaw 40 quarters, or 10 years, of uninterrupted earnings growth during the 1980s and early 1990s. . . . The ace in Welch's hand was GE Capital. The conglomerate's financing arm owned around $200 billion of assets, ranging from commercial buildings and leased jets to stock warrants, that it could sell at short notice to offset weakness elsewhere in the company. . . . The goal was to smooth GE's earnings by offsetting any big quarterly gains that would be hard to top in the future and making up for any significant losses by liquidating assets, tweaking valuations, and moving money around."[23]

In a similar vein, companies can make choices about how they report profitability across a number of fronts depending on incentives. You can look at the example of General Motors. GM owned an IT outsourcing business, GME, of which GM itself was the largest customer. GM had a class of GM shares that tracked the performance of the outsourcing business until 1996, when it decided to convert and split off its GME tracking stock into Electronic Data Systems (EDS) shares, which would trade independently. GM had a choice: Should the contract between GME and GM be priced competitively, moving profit toward GM, which was capitalized at a fairly low price-to-earnings multiple? Or should GME get more attractive pricing, increasing profits for GME, which was capitalized at a higher level? GM owned a large stake in EDS and decided to pursue the latter strategy. It did not work out for shareholders; EDS traded at $57 at the time of the split in 1996 but at just $17 in 2003.[24]

Off-Balance-Sheet Entities

There are ways to move entire segments of business off the balance sheet—and cover up numbers that you would rather people didn't see. Enron was a poster child for this, and because of what happened there, hiding entities off the balance sheet is harder now than it used to be. Enron had entities that it effectively controlled but were officially separate from the company and not consolidated into the financial statements. Enron would engage in transactions with these entities that would make it appear that Enron was making a lot of money—but these were not arm's-length transactions, and the prices were not legitimate. Self-dealing like this has been used by companies to hide things for a long time.

Even if it is now harder to do this in the US, in some foreign countries, you might have a family that controls a particular public company but also has one or multiple private entities on the side. These entities can engage in transactions where the private, wholly owned companies benefit at the expense of the publicly owned company. Profits on the private side go to the family, while on the publicly held side, profits have to be shared with the shareholders, providing an incentive to drive cash toward the privately held companies rather than the public ones.

Hanergy Solar, a Chinese clean-energy manufacturer run by one of China's richest men, Li Hejun, was guilty of something like this. Hanergy's primary customer was also its majority owner, Hanergy Group Holdings, which decided to withhold payment. Hanergy Solar had terrific earnings, but they were sitting in accounts receivable, and the cash was never actually collected.[25] Oops. As the *Washington Post* wrote, "China's richest man might have been running a massive fraud."[26] It took seven years, but Hejun was eventually arrested in China in 2022.[27]

Rupert Murdoch has also made some transactions where you might well question whether they were for the benefit of the public shareholders or for his children—I discuss this more in the governance chapter.

Defined Benefit Pension Plans

Pension funds—and particularly defined benefit pension funds—are rife with opportunities to manipulate the numbers. You need to assume a particular discount rate, a rate of return, and a host of other numbers that get built into these plans. Companies will choose different numbers simply to show the results they want to show. You can choose an unrealistically high discount rate or rate of return and make the numbers look pretty good. Or you might choose more realistic numbers, and then the reported earnings won't look as good.

Research has found that companies "make particularly high return assumptions in periods leading up to the acquisition of other firms."[28] The "opportunistic use of assumed rates of return," one study found, "led to aggregate levels of overvaluation."[29] Or you can do something even easier. In 2004, aerospace defense giant Raytheon simply changed the time it measured the value of its pension plan from December to October in order to artificially inflate earnings.[30]

Currency Manipulation

Here is a trick I have seen with multinational companies: if there are vastly different interest rates in different countries they operate in, they can put their liabilities in countries with low interest rates so that they pay less interest but invest their assets in countries with high rates of interest. The problem is that the currencies can adjust, and if the relative values of the currencies adjust suddenly, you might end up with a real problem. There can be earnings to show if this happens to work in one quarter—but they'll be erased (plus more) if the currencies move in an adverse way in the next quarter.

Changing Business Models

Companies can also change business models to affect accounting results. A great example of this is when, in the 1980s, IBM moved from a lease model to a sales model.[31] Under a leasing model, revenues and earnings are recognized over the life of the lease, with a customer providing revenue every year. When you switch to a sales model, you may have the same number of customers, but all earnings are realized in the year the sales transaction takes place, with no revenue coming in the future unless the customer buys a new piece of machinery. This accelerates present earnings and revenues at the expense of future earnings. Indeed, IBM's rate of revenue growth accelerated to a point where it was said to be heading toward $100 billion. But the acceleration was only temporary. Once leasing was reduced to minimal levels and customers had been converted to the sales model, the rate of growth returned to where it had been before, driven only by customer growth and not accounting sleight of hand.

The reverse maneuver has been used recently by a number of software companies, moving from a sales model to a subscription model. Some of this has been dictated by the way software is currently sold. It used to be that you purchased a box which had the software on CDs, along with a paper manual. Now, most software is sold online in the form of downloads, and people are used to a monthly charge model that gets them the latest features right away through online upgrades.

Moving from a sales model to a subscription model acts in the exact opposite direction from the IBM situation, lowering current revenue in order to ensure a steady stream of revenue in the future. This has created some opportunities to purchase software companies at unreasonably low valuations while they are in the process of converting from a sales model to a subscription model and their revenue appears artificially low. Adobe and Microsoft are examples of companies where this opened up great opportunities for long-term investors.

A similar thing happened with the Swedish telecommunications giant Ericsson. When cell phone service was evolving from analog to digital, Ericsson made the bold decision to increase R&D expenses in order to advance its digital transition. Just like the conversion from sales to subscription, this lowered current earnings but made it possible for future earnings to be significantly higher. Shortsighted investors, not understanding this potential, punished the company, and the stock price dropped—providing a terrific buying opportunity and bearing fruit once the transition was complete and revenue jumped.

Merger Accounting

Some of the biggest issues can occur around mergers—as all sorts of assumptions need to be made about the new company, and all kinds of accounting choices need to be reconciled because the two companies almost surely didn't make all the same reporting decisions. The potential for manipulating earnings increases astronomically in a merger. This is only exacerbated by the reality (discussed more in the management chapter) that a lot of mergers don't work out very well and that, on average, they are value-destructive.

Part of the problem emerges from the fact that when a company decides to sell itself, there may well be a good reason for it. It may realize its own accounting choices are about to catch up with it and future numbers are not going to look good. I have a deep suspicion that Monsanto sold itself to Bayer in 2018 because the company knew that the cancer lawsuits over its Roundup product were getting serious. Monsanto sold at a good price, and then the lawsuits started receiving some very big judgments. Had the company reserved appropriately? Almost surely not.

When a company offloads part of its business, there are many ways to manipulate the accounting statements. Perhaps you sell a particular business, but you decide it is not a material sale, so you don't have to break it out as a separate transaction. You can then use it to prop up operating earnings. At this point, you are basically deciding what that piece of the company was worth and how to record it in your books, and the decisions you make can drastically change what investors will perceive.

We can return once again to the egregious fraud of Waste Management, which acquired 441 companies over two years and collected a list of "one-time charges" against income. These special charges were ignored when considering profitability, so the stock did not suffer.[32]

The SEC caught the company CUC—a membership-based consumer services conglomerate—doing much the same thing. The company overstated merger and purchase reserves and then reversed the reserves, putting the money into operating expenses and artificially inflating profits. "In general," wrote the SEC, "the managers simply created whatever entries were needed to accomplish their goals, regardless of whether the entries were in any way grounded in the fiscal or business realities of CUC. . . . Other entries were intentionally created in odd amounts to hide the fact that the entries were completely fictitious. When merger reserves were initially established, amounts were routinely and intentionally overstated. At times, reversals of merger reserves were designated as revenues. As noted, the quarterly consolidated financial statements were largely fictional."[33]

Valuation of Derivatives

Years ago, National Energy Group, a subsidiary of PG&E, filed for bankruptcy. In the aftermath, it was discovered that National Energy had a large portfolio of derivatives. And, unfortunately, derivatives are never worth the amount that they're put on the books for. Traders of derivatives are paid based on how successful the trades are, so they make trades, and sometimes those trades are value-destructive, but they're accounted for as value-accretive so that the trader gets paid his bonus. This leads to a problem in the end, when you actually have to value the company. The value simply doesn't match what the books indicate. Thus, bankruptcy, and, for the investors, a lesson learned.

Asbestos and Environmental Liabilities

Thousands upon thousands of personal injury claims related to asbestos have lingered for decades, even though the use of asbestos largely ended (in the US) in the early 1970s. Even today, there are an estimated three thousand claims per year, with more than one hundred law firms filing claims, and some firms filing hundreds of claims each year.[34] The total cost of asbestos compensation has been estimated to reach more than $200 billion.[35]

This was, at one point, an enormous area of concern, and it remains an issue even for companies today. Many have not adequately reserved funds, and it then becomes an accounting risk. It is, however, relatively easy to research: either a company made or used asbestos products or it didn't. Yet some analysts fail to take heed. A similar issue exists with Superfund liability. It was relatively easy to determine who was exposed to risk based on the nature of a business and the kinds of chemicals that may have been involved. Superfund lawsuits have a joint and several liability aspect to them so that if one particular company can be shown to have contributed to a problem, it could be responsible for the entire cost of the cleanup. This creates significant risk worth examining. The problem of PFAS—per- and polyfluoroalkyl substances, also known as "forever chemicals" that are used in nonstick cookware—is another example. In 2023, 3M agreed to pay $10.3 billion to settle future lawsuits related to these compounds. [36]

ESG Factors

It has become trendy over the past generation—and especially over the past few years—to incorporate environmental, social, and governance (ESG) factors into the analysis of a company when deciding whether to invest, and, indeed, there has been an incredible amount of pressure on investors to consider these issues quite strongly. Of course, governance issues are critical to pay attention to, and we will spend an entire chapter on governance later in the book. Environmental concerns are also critical to evaluate, particularly in the case of companies with real liabilities that have been underreserved (thus making earnings look higher since sufficient money has not been set aside). And social concerns that can lead to problems for a company going forward—as with any concern that might cause issues to arise in the future—should never be ignored.

The problem here, however, is more nuanced. On the one hand, these issues are, of course, important to individuals and to society. On the other hand, environmental and social issues can mean different things to different people, and the metrics that have been created to evaluate companies on the basis of ESG factors often do not agree on which companies are strong and which companies are weak. When pressured to rely on these metrics, what an investor ought to do can depend more on the metric than on reality. How can investors align their investments to satisfy ESG concerns if there isn't even agreement as to what those concerns are? In an environment where information is confusing, it becomes critical to do your own analysis—does the company in question actually have an issue set to cause problems down the road? You can't merely rely on a third-party score that may be driven by political factors or other concerns that do not match the reality of the situation.

There is particular confusion when it comes to environmental rankings. Some environmental issues are quite clear cut, like asbestos and Superfund issues, as discussed in the previous section. A chemical company will almost certainly have environmental liabilities that are not carried on its balance sheet. If it ever tried to close its plants, there would surely be significant (and likely unreserved) cleanup costs associated. This is true for oil refiners as well. Chemicals and the byproducts of oil refining almost certainly leak into the ground. This happens all the time and is very expensive to clean up. Investors must be aware of these unstated liabilities; I believe the government will eventually require cleanup, and you don't want to be an investor in a business that suddenly has billions of dollars in liabilities that you were not aware of.

Similarly, I don't think there's ever been a nuclear plant decommissioned within the reserve level of the nuclear decommissioning trusts that are set up to handle these issues. The companies all need to have these trust funds, but the actual decommissioning ends up costing far more. And management has an incentive to underreserve.

A lot of people are also now concerned about carbon dioxide emissions, for good reason—but that is a much more complicated subject that leads to disagreement. Which companies are creating carbon dioxide, and which companies are not creating carbon dioxide? We can look, for example, at Apple. Apple typically ranks very highly as a company not creating much carbon dioxide—but the reality is that a lot of Apple's manufacturing is subcontracted, and there's a large amount of carbon dioxide being generated in the making of an iPhone or a Mac. Since Apple doesn't participate directly in the high–carbon dioxide elements, the company is not penalized by rankings. This may not actually make sense. If restrictions are put in place, its business will surely be affected; hence, the issue ought to be on the radar of any potential investor.

There are lawsuits in Europe, as another example of ESG risk, relating to carbon dioxide discharge. In June 2023, airlines in Europe were sued for making potentially misleading claims about the sustainability of flying and the airlines' contributions to carbon emissions.[37] Whenever there are plausible environmental concerns in a company's business, the risk of downstream liability should always be carefully considered.

Similarly, electric car manufacturers are given a lot of credit when it comes to environmental issues, but some people make the case that electric cars are a huge environmental problem because the materials being mined to make the batteries have many environmental consequences associated with them. Then there is the further issue of where the electricity that is being used to charge the cars is coming from. If you are charging the car using coal-derived electricity, the car could actually be emitting more carbon dioxide than a gasoline-powered car. Alternatively, you could use solar power, and then it would be quite clean. So there are a lot of different ways to look at carbon dioxide emissions, and it is just not as simple as it may seem at first glance, or as a numerical ranking may make it appear.

Even in companies that initially look quite problematic from a carbon dioxide point of view, the truth is not always that straightforward. Occidental Petroleum is an interesting example. The company is in the oil-producing business, so some people would instinctively say that this is terrible and that they are contributing to global warming because they are making gasoline. But Occidental has also developed a technology over the years for pulling carbon dioxide out of the air. The company initially developed it to inject carbon dioxide into oil wells in order to produce more oil, but the technology is quite advanced and can also be used to pull carbon dioxide out of the air and put it into the ground, where it would remain permanently. In this sense, Occidental actually has green bona fides. Removing carbon dioxide from the air is probably going to become necessary at some point, and Occidental has highly developed technology to do just that. This example shows that it is hard to look at a company and immediately know where it stands with respect to environmental issues.

This example also shows why blanket exclusions are generally not a good idea if you are looking for investments that will be long-term sustainable successes. You need to look at the individual facts and circumstances. Occidental's carbon-capture technology could be a hugely profitable element of its business going forward, but if you say you don't want to own any energy companies, you would throw Occidental out rather than reap the potential future rewards (and encourage green efforts going forward). Holcim, a global manufacturer of building materials such as concrete, is another example. On its face, the company is a high carbon emitter, but its commitment to sustainability makes it a better choice in this respect than its alternatives.[38] Looking merely at emissions and not the alternative possibilities can blind you to the reality of the situation.

Moving beyond the environment, the social part of ESG can be problematic as well. You want to invest in companies that generally have good labor relations, and the reality is that if a company doesn't care for its community, the community will probably take it out on the company at some level, so you want to find companies that behave in responsible and sustainable ways. But beyond those issues, there is a lot of politics informing the social aspect of ESG ratings, and the result is rankings that are not necessarily aligned with someone looking for a quality long-term investment result.

Just as an example, there may be some people who think abortion is a right and others who think it is a mortal sin—so where a company stands on that issue is going to be offensive to some and not to others. That can apply to many different issues. Some of the rating services will rate a company higher if it has a union, but a union can often be destructive to shareholder value over a long period of time, so it is not necessarily the case that a powerful union is the friend of an investor. It becomes very hard, especially in a politically charged environment, to understand what actually leads to a company having a positive social impact in a way that benefits a long-term investor.

Even on governance issues, different people can rate the same company very differently. What's important to the rater can vary quite widely: some people think that an independent chair is a great idea; some think a majority of independent directors is sufficient. There is, of course, reasoning for these preferences, but you need to dig deeper into the details. As we will discuss in the governance chapter, it really comes down to whether the management and directors are actually incentivized to create long-term sustainable success for the organization or just short-term profit, or perhaps other goals misaligned with long-term success.

The ultimate issue around ESG—and why it is hard to turn ratings into actionable steps—is that it is very hard as an investor, even an investor who owns a significant percentage of a company, to force action of any kind on a board or management team that is not interested. If you're an institutional investor who owns as much as 5, 10, or 15 percent of a company, certainly, at that level, the CEO will return your calls and you can have meetings with outside directors, but your ability to actually influence what a company is doing is very limited. One would need, at a minimum, to have an activist involved, and a group of large shareholders has to be in general agreement concerning the goals of the activist.

Activists who are successful are typically either pressing for the breakup of a company, selling it off in pieces, or interested in selling the whole company. Of course, this is quite threatening to the people in charge. There are activist organizations that will try to pursue change, some of them union-driven, railing against excess compensation for the management team, with the real goal being to unionize the company. There are an increasing number of people who are concerned with carbon emissions, so they make various proposals, but a lot of those fail, lacking sufficient votes—and it isn't always clear that the environmental activists are driven by the idea of benefiting the long-term shareholder.

The reality is that changing the behavior of, say, an oil company isn't always good for investors. It's not clear that existing oil companies would have a competitive advantage when you move away from fossil fuels. They may just be throwing away shareholder money if they pursue wind or solar or some other kind of clean energy solution when they aren't really suited to pursue those solutions. There's something to be said for investing in some of the smaller energy companies that aren't being pressured to look at alternatives to the same extent as the larger firms. Those smaller firms can pursue their core businesses without distraction. That's not to say that it isn't good if the world moves toward cleaner energy—but the way to pursue that goal may not involve long-term investors pressuring existing companies to change their business models.

Fraud

Finally, we get to issues that go beyond accounting manipulation, choices, reserves, and other considerations into outright fraud. In the United States and the developed countries, we rarely see instances of outright fraud today, but it is common in the emerging markets, where there may be less ethical business climates. We can look at the Satyam Computer Services scandal, at one point India's largest corporate fraud, as an example of where it's beyond clear that a line was crossed. According to the SEC, the company "used false invoices and forged bank statements to inflate the company's cash balances and make it appear far more profitable to investors."[39] In fact, the company reported cash holdings of more than $1 billion that, according to *Forbes*, "simply did not exist."[40] Auditors actually signed off on these reports, making it even more incomprehensible.

The Chinese poultry company Yuhe International suffered from a similar scandal. It reported a $15 million acquisition of thirteen broiler breeder farms . . . which never happened.[41] The company launched an IPO based on the strength of this fictional acquisition, ultimately getting delisted from NASDAQ.[42]

These aren't just examples where someone made an indefensible judgment about how long to depreciate equipment, but where they, in fact, made up wild and completely false information. These are both situations where companies got caught, but I suspect there are many, many more instances where people aren't caught. The sad truth is that people do sometimes get away with these things, and once you get away with something small, the temptation is to go bigger and bigger. Once you start down that road and become a little corrupt, you can quickly become a lot more corrupt. There have actually been a number of frauds where a company started out with a small trading loss and people tried to cover it up, figuring that at some point they would earn enough to pay it back—and then the loss just got bigger and bigger, eventually leading to complete disaster.

Nick Leeson was the twenty-eight-year-old head of derivatives in Singapore for Barings Bank, the oldest merchant bank in the United Kingdom. From 1992 until 1995, he made increasingly risky unauthorized trades and eventually singlehandedly bankrupted the bank.[43] His job had been arbitrage, generating small profits from buying and selling futures contracts in the Osaka Securities Exchange and the Singapore International Monetary Exchange. Instead, he tried to make even bigger profits—and initially succeeded, earning the bank over £10 million in 1992. Later, when his trades went bad, he hid the losses in a secret internal account. There were no checks on these trades; he was the person assigned to review his own activity. Eventually, in the wake of an overnight earthquake that caused the Asian markets to plunge in January 1995, the losses were too much to paper over. Making increasingly risky trades as he attempted to make back the money, Leeson ended up losing $1.4 billion for the bank, double what they even had available to trade.[44]

Leeson went a full month before being caught, eventually leaving an apology note and fleeing Singapore. He was found and sentenced to six and a half years in jail.[45] He now works as, of all things, an investigator of financial misdeeds.[46]

Then, of course, there is Bernie Madoff, who ended up running a $65 billion Ponzi scheme and losing money "invested" by more than twenty-four thousand victims. Madoff had a market-making business that was legitimate, and then, for some reason, he just started venturing into bigger and bigger fraud. If someone is corruptible at some level, they can decide they see an opportunity and end up going further and further with it.

Shockingly (perhaps), three researchers have estimated that 11 percent of large, publicly traded US corporations are committing fraud every year.[47] I am confident that outside the United States, the numbers are even higher, especially in countries that have known corruption challenges, particularly in emerging markets. Fraud is a cyclical phenomenon. When securities valuations are very high, the incentive to commit fraud goes up. A fraudulent dollar of earnings is worth far more in a 30-times multiple environment than when there is a 10-times multiple. Fraud tends to get committed when equity valuations are high and the economy is strong. Note that the huge frauds concerning Enron, Computer

Associates, and WorldCom (whose fraud was similar to CUC in some ways, creating reserves and then feeding them back into earnings[48]) all happened during the internet bubble. Fraud tends to be uncovered when times become more difficult. This is partly because it becomes harder to sustain fraud in the face of a weaker economy, and the incentives to sustain it weaken with lower valuations. I truly believe that fraud is a very difficult thing to succeed at over a long period of time. As more and more people are exposed to the fraud, the likelihood of being able to continue it without being discovered diminishes.

So what can we do to look for fraud? The first place to look is at the auditors. Auditors sign off on a company's financial statements and should be the first line of defense against fraud. True fraud almost inevitably requires a conspiracy with the auditors because it's very hard to completely dupe competent auditors if they're actually trying to do their jobs. The presence of a high-quality, large audit firm conveys some comfort. However, one must look closely even when large, reputable audit firms are involved. Ask the question, Does the auditor provide other services to the client?

We have seen situations, such as with Arthur Andersen and Enron, where the audit firm will sell other services to the audit client, with a lot of money changing hands. The bigger the number, the more problematic the relationship can become. You can get to a point where a client says it wants a certain expense or transaction treated in a certain way, and the auditor may push back and say this goes against generally accepted accounting principles (GAAP)—but if there is a lot of money involved, the audit firm doesn't want to lose the client, and the conflict is more likely to get resolved in the company's favor.

One thing you can do is compare the level of audit fees to those at comparable companies and see if the fees in this circumstance are outsized in any way. That can provide a bit of a clue.

Obviously, this problem is even more likely when the audit firm is very small relative to the company being audited. If the audit firm has one giant client compared to the rest of its business, the audit firm will probably do what the giant client says because it will be out of business if it loses that client. Small audit firms are particularly suspect in situations involving a large, established company. There is likely a reason the company didn't choose to go with one of the major players, and that reason may well be that it is hiding fraudulent activity. So you have to be especially suspicious of small, untested audit firms, even if it's also true that the big firms aren't necessarily 100 percent reliable.

Investors in the Italy-based dairy company Parmalat suffered because of exactly this. For years, the company committed a range of types of fraud, creating fake assets, hiding debt from investors, and double billing.[49] They even forged the signature of a Bank of America employee on a document that was actually reviewed by their auditors, but was not flagged as a problem. The only reason the fraud was uncovered is that under Italian law, the company was required to switch auditors every nine years.[50] The old auditor, in fact, conspired with executives to hide the fraud from the new auditor. But the new auditor caught on and ultimately found that the CEO and sixteen (!) other executives had misappropriated over €1 billion.[51] The company eventually reached a settlement of €357 million and is now a subsidiary of the French dairy giant Lactalis.

An occasional change of auditors is arguably a good thing. There is judgment in accounting, and a fresh set of eyes may see things differently. But a frequent change of auditors can signal that a firm's accounting is seriously compromised. Companies that keep firing auditors until a compliant one is found are, of course, likely to be doing something quite suspect. Rapid change in auditors for no apparent reason merits further investigation.

Along these lines, I've always found the idea that anyone gave money to Bernie Madoff to be quite amazing. First, if something seems too good to be true—in this case, impossibly high, stable returns through all investing environments—it almost surely is. Second, if you look at legitimate money managers, the funds are custodied at State Street or another custodian bank. Madoff custodied his own funds, so there wasn't a bank holding the actual securities or an independent set of eyes doing the accounting. His auditor was a firm run by his brother-in-law, and Madoff's niece was the firm's compliance officer. So there was a fundamental problem with both the custody and the auditing, which should have been a red flag to anyone exploring an investment.

Particularly as I've gotten older, I've realized that if you see absolutely any signs of fraud at all, the only solution is to run away. A person's character doesn't change. If someone is willing to be a little corrupt, he is probably willing to be a lot corrupt. Your risk tolerance here should be very, very low. Untrustworthy management should be avoided at all costs. Investors do get caught up in short-term thinking and can miss signs that look obvious in hindsight, or perhaps sometimes they are just blind to the truth, especially when focused on fears or worries. People start wondering if we are going into a recession or get caught up in short-term predictions about how things will unfold and start searching for quick bargains or places to make fast returns. They stop looking at things like governance, the alignment of the management team with long-term shareholders, the accounting quality, or simply whether people are telling the truth and have sound moral character, and they end up investing in things that are outright scams. If you are a long-term investor, you can't chase quick returns. You always have to keep your eye on the long-term outcomes because your ability to guess what's going to happen year to year is absolutely unreliable.

Forecasting is really hard, but forecasting isn't really the game. What generates long-term earnings isn't based on guesswork; it's based on real information like a company's competitive position, their compensation structure, and everything else to be discussed in the pages that follow.

Quantitative Indicators of Concern

Aside from looking at the auditors, there are two quantitative tools I wanted to mention, both of which can be useful in evaluating a company's numbers. One tool that can be used to detect outright fraud is Benford's Law. Benford's Law concerns how often digits tend to be distributed in large number datasets. It happens that leading digits have small values far more often than they have large ones—it is more than six times likelier for a number to start with a one than with a nine.[52]

When people fudge numbers, they tend not to be aware of this and don't track these frequencies—and the distribution is noticeably off. Sometimes, if there is a particular limit on a type of transaction, fraudulent actors will keep many transactions just below that threshold value. Benford's Law can help establish whether a set of numbers is questionable and determine a likelihood of fraud just based on the distribution of numbers and ratios.

Professor M. Daniel Beneish of Indiana University created another model to help detect if a company is likely to have manipulated its earnings. The model takes eight pieces of data from financial statements—gross margin index, asset quality index, and others—and calculates a ratio from these numbers that indicates the likelihood that earnings have been manipulated.[53] It was used, most notably, to find fraud at Enron before the scandal there revealed the truth.

Even when there are no accounting issues, there are, of course, so many other factors to consider when deciding whether something makes sense as a long-term investment. In the next chapter, we will look at franchise and how to evaluate the inherent merits of a business.

CHAPTER 3
FRANCHISE

When I talk about franchise, I'm referring to something broader in scope than what we mean when we talk about *franchising*, or licensing a particular business to operate in a certain territory. I'm talking about the nuts and bolts of a business and whether or not it makes sense to enter a particular market, in a particular industry, with a particular product or service, given the other businesses, products, and services that already exist and given the population of potential buyers. The big question of this chapter is how to evaluate a business beyond its management, the accounting choices it makes, or the ups and downs it is likely to experience simply because of broader market or societal trends. Underneath all that, is this business, in and of itself, well-positioned for long-term success, or are there reasons to doubt?

It is clear that the ideal company from this perspective would be a monopoly in a space where there are lots of suppliers, lots of customers, no competition, and high barriers to entry. Of course, we almost never find all those characteristics at once, and often we find none of them. But the closer to this ideal a business can get, the better-positioned it is to thrive over time. Conversely, when you encounter businesses with a limited number of suppliers, a limited number of customers, or lots of competitors, you need to ask yourself, Where is this business's leverage? How can it maintain a healthy profit and earn back money for its investors? If there are lots of competitors, it is hard to find any kind of pricing advantage, either from suppliers or in selling to customers. Most businesses that are in highly competitive markets never earn back their cost of capital, so it is very difficult for them to make money over time. They may make money during an economic upcycle, but they will give it all back in an economic downcycle, so their ability to earn solid returns over the long run is very limited.

Considering franchise value has proven to be quite important throughout my career. I did an analysis some years ago on the companies with strong franchises that I made the mistake of selling too soon. There was the paint company, Sherwin-Williams, that had a strong brand and a powerful channel for professional users, along with significant pricing power; there was Adobe/Autodesk, with highly differentiated products that millions of designers relied upon for their livelihood and many opportunities to continue to improve their product features over the long term; there were companies in the electronic design automation (EDA) market, which consolidated over time and left the industry leaders in a strong position for growth. There is also value in sitting between two markets and enabling them both to function more effectively. Think about Google and Facebook connecting advertisers to enormous networks of users. The power of long-term compounding growth should lead investors to pay strong attention to structurally superior franchises because they are likely to pay off over time. What follows are some factors to be considered when analyzing franchises.

Competitor Concentration

Lots of competitors usually means a poor chance of solid returns, but you need to also recognize that industries aren't static forever. One thing you can look for in the market is industries that may be hypercompetitive now but are in the process of consolidating. There are absolutely situations where industries change over time, turning previously poor investments into solid ones. As an example, at one time, there were several dynamic random-access memory (DRAM) chip manufacturers, and it was a terrible business. In good times, people made money, but it wasn't sustainable in economic downturns. And then, the industry began to consolidate.

It ended up coming down to three large manufacturers, Samsung, Micron, and SK Hynix, holding 94 percent of the market by 2021,[1] and that consolidation made the market much better for investors. The raw material—the equipment needed to make DRAM—is sand, which is widely available. And there are lots of customers for DRAM across technology, automotive, and other industries. So it is a well-positioned business from those angles, but when there were lots of competitors, there was cutthroat pricing, and no one could make good money. As soon as the industry consolidated, things changed. The big players knew that if they cut the price, they would be hurting themselves just as much as they would hurt their competitors, so they were incentivized not to do it. This does not mean there aren't still ups and downs—there certainly are—but what saves the market is that with fewer competitors who might overinvest on capacity during a cyclical upturn and compete fiercely on price, the market can more readily absorb excess capacity, and the "good times" are actually good for the companies, making up for the down cycles.

Important to note here is that not all competitors are equal. It may be okay to have a large number of competitors if those competitors are hampered in some way—say, state-owned banks in India losing share because private banks are typically better at deciding to whom to extend credit, or any business where incumbents might need to reprice the base in order to compete with new entrants (cable television or cell phone companies, for instance).

Labor Concentration

The concentration of labor is also a factor that affects a business. Labor unions achieve their maximum benefit when they can monopolize labor in a particular industry, or at least come close. One of the most successful unions covered the US auto industry, where United Auto Workers (UAW) created huge benefits for workers—and costs to companies—for many years. When US consumers began buying more cars from foreign manufacturers, the foreign manufacturers weren't represented by UAW, and so, in many cases, they had far lower labor costs. This put a lot of pressure on US manufacturers, and, in my view, eventually led to the purchase of American Motors by Chrysler, and later to the bankruptcy of Chrysler and General Motors.

If just one competitor is being unionized, the union can't really raise the wage rate above what other companies are paying. But if a union can create a monopoly for itself, then wages can be escalated quite effectively.

The reverse happens when there is a breakup of a unionized industry. A situation like this has played out with taxicabs. This was a heavily regulated business for a long time, with taxicab driver unions ensuring certain wage levels. This was not necessarily for the benefit of consumers, with high prices, low availability of cabs, and the generally poor physical conditions of taxicabs. The introduction of competition in the form of Uber and Lyft devastated the whole labor market. Unions came under great pressure because Uber and Lyft had much lower labor costs and were driving prices down. Suddenly, the taxicab medallions in cities like New York and San Francisco were not worth nearly what owners had paid, and the industry broke down.

Customer Concentration

It is risky for companies when there are very few customers for their products, even when those customers are large and making significant purchases. Another example from the tech space: there used to be a robust disk drive industry. Sales were strong, but if you looked beneath the surface, you would realize that there were very few independent buyers. Only a few computer companies existed to purchase these disk drives, so the suppliers were very much at risk. They couldn't afford to lose any of their customers because each one was responsible for so much of their business. If a customer that accounts for 20 percent or 30 percent of a company's sales threatens to leave, the company will do almost anything to keep it, including cutting the price. A limited number of customers means that those customers have too much leverage over the supplier. Two or three big customers for disk drives accounted for 80 percent of the market, so these buyers had all the power. This effectively approaches a monopsony situation, where there is only one buyer and thus the buyer can set the price.

In the end, these turn out to be poor investment opportunities. Auto parts is a similar type of industry. There are more car manufacturers than computer manufacturers, but it is still a very limited number. Auto parts manufacturers may have four or five big companies—and each of them doesn't necessarily service all the car models that exist—so they are really at the mercy of their customers.

On the flip side, if you are looking at one of the customers in a situation like this, you can often find a really good and investable business. Walmart is incredibly strong because it can beat up on its suppliers. The bigger it has gotten, the more power the company has earned in the marketplace, to the point where it can insist on price breaks and other special deals. Walmart often accounts for 15–20 percent of the sales of certain consumer products, so it has a lot of leverage if it threatens to drop the product from its stores. Walmart ends up getting concessions and buying its goods cheaper than anyone else. Thus, it can sell its products to customers for less than its competitors can and still make the same profit margin. That is a huge advantage, and the bigger Walmart gets, the more of an advantage it becomes. It's a virtuous cycle for Walmart, as more and more customers come for the lower and lower prices.

If a company has the leverage to beat up its suppliers—especially when their competitors don't have that same leverage—it can make for a terrific opportunity. And, conversely, if there is a limited number of suppliers, those suppliers can earn a lot of money because their customers are at their mercy. As the graph that follows illustrates, as the semiconductor industry consolidated, it moved to much higher levels of profitability.[2] Preconsolidation, over time, the net margin fluctuated between positive and negative numbers, and the industry struggled to earn a lot of money.

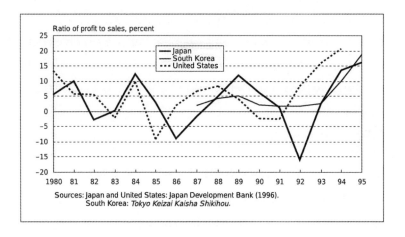

Sources: Japan and United States: Japan Development Bank (1996). South Korea: *Tokyo Keizai Kaisha Shikihou.*

Economies of Scale

The Walmart example points to a broader idea about economies of scale. The bigger a company gets, the cheaper the products should be as the company gains more leverage over suppliers. The idea of lower costs as you grow bigger makes a company an effective economy-of-scale business. A lot of manufacturing businesses are like this by nature. The more they make, the lower the average cost, simply because so much of the expense is in the fixed cost of equipment and factories, which doesn't increase as you sell more goods (at least until you need to build more factories or buy more equipment).

This is where mergers can have positive effects (as opposed to the many mergers that fail to create value). If you take two companies that are in the same business and combine them to end up with a lower unit cost of production, you can become much more profitable. Similarly, if a company that has a distribution channel can buy a company that has a product it can sell through that channel, you create a situation where the acquirer does not have to invest anything in the business but can simply use its own channel to pump more product through. Cisco Systems used this acquisition strategy successfully in its earlier years. The situation becomes a cost savings, and a merger like this can make a lot of sense.

Not all mergers take advantage of these effects, of course. I look at mergers such as AT&T buying Time Warner in 2018 as an example of an acquisition that created no real economy-of-scale effects because the firms had nothing in common. The telephone executives had no grasp of the movie business, and they believed a story about the convergence of technology and entertainment that was not based in fact. The phone company needed reliability and billing expertise. The movie business is a creative one that requires none of those same skills. Instead of mergers like these, you want to see businesses decide to buy their smaller competitors.

I have come across a lot of savvy businesspeople who understood this. There was one ruthless CEO of a Japanese company who was obsessive about dominating a particular niche market. He either drove his competitors out of business or purchased them, and once he was done buying them out, he moved on to purchase the companies that made the parts he needed, understanding that not only would this help his own business but he could also stop selling those needed parts to the few competitors he still had and thus become even more dominant in the industry. In the end, he went even further and established a school designed to train future workers—for his business and no others. He saw it as a charitable enterprise to give back to the community by letting people train to work for him and him alone. Of course, given that he was dominating the space more and more, perhaps it was indeed charitable to keep people from working for competitors that would soon no longer exist.

This is an extreme version of the kind of mentality you absolutely want to see in a CEO. You want people who are incredibly focused on taking over a growth business and finding ways to grow it, lowering costs and increasing profits along the way.

Economies of scale can play out in different ways. Pharmaceutical companies see a clear relationship between size and profitability. Part of this is that they have distribution networks in place, and you can use the same networks to sell your products, whether you have one drug on the market or five hundred of them.

You have to build those networks and relationships regardless, so the incremental cost of distributing one more drug is much lower. See the following figure from Bain and Company showing this relationship.[3]

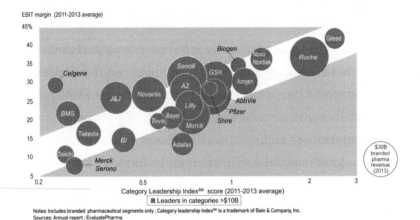

EBIT margin (2011-2013 average)

Category Leadership Index℠ score (2011-2013 average)

■ Leaders in categories >$10B

$30B branded pharma revenue (2013)

Notes: Includes branded pharmaceutical segments only ; Category leadership Index℠ is a trademark of Bain & Company, Inc.
Sources: Annual report ; EvaluatePharma

The cell phone business is like this as well. Costs are relatively fixed for cellular service providers, so market share governs profitability. You need to put the towers in place to cover a particular geography, and then the more customers you have, the better. In virtually every market around the world, we see the same pattern: the market leader makes a good profit, the number-two player makes an okay profit, the number-three player is marginally profitable, and beyond that, any other entrants are decidedly unprofitable.

Locked-In Customer Bases

We can go one step further with the idea of economies of scale to a related discussion about locked-in customer bases. Market shares can be difficult to change once companies establish their relative positions in a particular space. Once you are the cell phone leader in a particular geography, for example, you can offer lower prices so customers are disinclined to change. Same for Walmart: If its prices are lower, why would a customer move to a competitor?

But a locked-in customer base is a separate point in some other examples. Certain businesses are simply easier or harder spaces in which to move a customer from one vendor to another. There is a degree of pain in switching that is different in every industry. For instance, it is not difficult at all for a commodity buyer to switch purely based on price. But other businesses are not so straightforward. Once someone gets used to her cell phone provider, it is unlikely she will move without tremendous reason because switching her phone, her plan, and potentially her phone number all create huge disincentives to change. (The FCC's decision in 2003 to require number portability, where users could switch carriers but keep their phone number, led to an uptick in churn because someone would no longer lose their phone number if they switched to a cheaper provider.)

Banks are the same way. You may have a banking relationship for years and not be terribly motivated to change unless something dramatic happens. The cost of switching is very significant for an individual in a banking relationship. On the other hand, the cost for a corporation, which is dealing in much larger dollar amounts, is relatively small, and companies have systems in place for changing vendors. Thus, in the banking business, individuals are a much better market to target than corporations, or at least they are a more reliable one. (Though the recent case of First Republic luring high-net-worth retail customers serves as a counterexample, despite ultimately leading to the bank's downfall.[4])

It can be similar in other industries. Social networks are another important one to consider. It is hard to recreate one's network on a new platform. When looking at businesses, the pain of customers switching should be considered quite significantly.

Patents and Copyrights

Another potential set of barriers to entry involves patents and copyrights. A company having these can keep competitors out of the market, and they ought to be valued quite significantly when looking at a business. One of the most famous situations here happened back in the 1980s when Intel decided not to license its design for the 386 computer microprocessor to other manufacturers. Intel had allowed others to make the 286 microprocessor, and by allowing multiple sources, its chips had become embedded in IBM and IBM-compatible PCs under the theory that more sources meant more production and the company wouldn't be limited by its own inability to meet demand. For the 386, Intel decided to go sole-source and was able to increase the price tremendously. The former SVP and general counsel of Intel, Tom Dunlap, has said, "I look at it as a game of chicken . . . . 186, 286, they won. 386, we didn't blink. We said, 'Okay, we're not going to give the

386 away. We understand there may be some customer problems. We'll build another facility. We'll work with our customers. We're going to make that work.'"[5]

And it did, leading to a massive increase in Intel's margin and huge expansion. There was a large increase in revenue and net income during the transition, as you can see in the diagram that follows.[6]

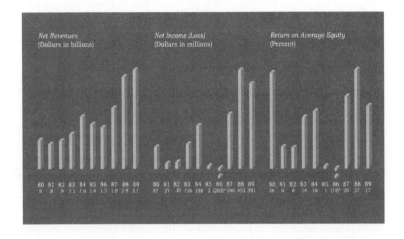

The company used its ownership of the copyright on the 386 chip as a huge advantage. Eventually, other companies (AMD, most notably) found ways to engineer around the problem and make compatible chips that didn't violate Intel's intellectual property, but for a period of time, Intel effectively had a license to print money.

Natural Monopolies

Barriers to entry can also emerge from natural monopolies. In the case of electricity distribution, you can't really get out of buying your power through the local electric distributor because there simply isn't another set of wires coming into your house. The same is true for cable television. In most municipalities, there is one set of cables coming into your house, and that is what you have to use. Interestingly, this type of monopoly doesn't exist in Europe, where they have a number of integrated communications companies that wire homes—and what we can notice as a result is that the cable companies in the US are considerably more profitable than in Europe, where there's competition.

This outsized profit has been undermined in the US in recent years as the phone companies have laid fiber-optic cable into people's homes, making these phone companies extremely competitive with local cable companies—not to mention there is also the competitive threat from wireless technologies that keep improving. This point relates to technological change causing industry disruption, which is an issue I discuss in more detail. Nevertheless, there remain some natural monopolies that have not yet been disrupted. There is only one set of water pipes to people's homes, for instance. The government has in many cases regulated these natural monopolies, setting the rate of return for electric companies, for example, and making them more or less profitable in different states depending on the rules. You must evaluate the political environment in order to make a judgment about whether or not to invest in these companies. In California, there are two large electric utilities, PG&E and SoCal Edison.

They are affected quite significantly by the political environment, and their profits are limited. Other states have a more benign regulatory environment. Natural monopolies can be great businesses to invest in because they are not cyclical—people always need electricity, gas, and water—but if politicians limit the rate of return, they may not, in fact, rcmain as profitable.

Technology and Government Regulation

The biggest barrier to entry is, of course, scale, as we already discussed. But the benefits of scale can be undermined by changes in technology or government regulation. An example of this is Telmex, a company that used to dominate 90 percent of the telephone market in Mexico.[7] Owned by billionaire Carlos Slim, the company was able to use its market share to increase prices to the point where a long-distance call in Mexico was priced at a huge premium compared to long-distance calls in the US. Eventually, the Mexican government decided that the quasi-monopoly that it had allowed to exist had grown too powerful, and it tried to break up the business.

In these cases, governments can override the typical benefits that an economy of scale provides and make things very difficult for the market leader. We see this now in the US with the Federal Trade Commission suing Google over its dominance in the online advertising market.

It is not just the government; it is also technology. In Mexico, Telmex was affected not just by government regulation but also by the growth of cellular products and the fact that people were no longer tied to their landlines. Suddenly, the fact that Telmex was so dominant in the telephone market was far less relevant; the network the company had built could be disrupted by cellular companies coming in and gaining customers. Technology is often the driver of businesses being able to overcome even large barriers to entry. Take, for instance, Uber versus taxicabs, the PC versus mainframe computers, solid state media versus disk drives, and CDs versus cassette tapes as just a few examples.

Barriers to Exit

We often think about barriers to entry as factors to consider when evaluating a company's future potential, but sometimes we ignore barriers to exit that can be just as powerful in determining the fate of a business. Companies that sit on toxic waste sites face an interesting dilemma: while they are operating, they don't necessarily need to recognize or clean up the mess, but if they try to wrap up the business, it can be very expensive to address the issue. When General Motors filed for bankruptcy, this became an issue for investors. The company was able to get rid of the liabilities, but their security holders suffered.

As discussed earlier, companies often don't reserve appropriate funds to handle these end-of-life obligations. Nuclear plant decommissioning is one example already mentioned. It is a very expensive thing to do, rarely covered fully by reserves. A different issue: in many foreign countries (less so in the US), a large downsizing of the workforce can turn into a political issue that costs a company more money than expected. Winding up any facet of a large business can yield unforeseen expenses. General Electric attempted to spin off its long-term-care insurance business, but first it needed to increase reserves for future claims by billions of dollars.[8] Similarly, Deutsche Bank had difficulty winding up its derivatives business because there were a lot of long-term derivatives on the books.[9] Given the problem that derivatives portfolios are so often overvalued, Deutsche Bank couldn't get anyone else to take on the portfolio at anything close to the value at which the company was carrying them.

Unfunded health liabilities and defined benefit pension plans carry some of these same risks. They are almost always more expensive than allocated for, so companies end up with a real problem exiting businesses because of these costs.

Product Differentiation

Product differentiation is another important factor to keep an eye on. If your company is competing in a commodity business, it is hard to achieve any kind of differentiation between your products and others, so you can never gain real pricing power. We see this with aluminum and steel, or other products that simply are what they are. If someone else makes them and undercuts your price, they will get the business. What you want instead is to find companies that have highly differentiated products.

I see Microsoft as a tremendous example of this. When Microsoft moved from DOS to Windows, the company created a unique operating system that everyone wanted—and gave itself huge market leverage that ended up carrying along its other products, even those that may have been inferior to the competition. At the time that Windows launched, Microsoft did not have the leading spreadsheet or word processing programs. Lotus 1-2-3 was the leading spreadsheet, and WordPerfect was the leading word processor. But neither could adapt quickly enough to Windows, and since Microsoft was able to develop its competitor applications in house and know in advance the changes that would be needed in order to take best advantage of the latest Windows versions, it was able to keep Excel and Word ahead enough that they became dominant in their spaces. So Microsoft ended up not only winning with its operating system but also carrying along its other products to become highly differentiated winners themselves.

Granularity

We can also look at granularity, or the level of detail that a company takes into account in a decision-making process, and sometimes use this to our advantage in analyzing a business. A very interesting example is in the business of connectors for semiconductors. There is a set of companies, Molex among the leaders, that make the connectors used to link together expensive computer parts. The connectors themselves have a very low cost per unit. It's a giant economy-of-scale business. The semiconductors themselves might cost tens or even hundreds of dollars, but the connectors cost pennies. Manufacturers of the devices that need these connectors will focus much more on the cost of the semiconductors because a 50 percent jump would be astronomical on those products, but it is barely noticeable if a connector is fifteen cents instead of ten cents.

When a company is making an inexpensive product that goes with much more expensive parts, they can price quite aggressively because the buyers may simply not be paying enough attention to care. Molex's customers simply won't notice a significant increase in price, benefiting the company and its shareholders. This creates interesting pricing power for something vital yet very cheap to manufacture and sell.

Share versus Pricing

It is important to discuss the idea of share versus price. I have spent a lot of time in this chapter discussing market share, but sometimes management may decide that it is worth yielding some market share in order to raise prices and boost profitability, at least in the short term. Market share tends to move slowly, so this can be a good strategy for management to improve short-term results . . . but it creates huge risk in the long run. In the management chapter, I will discuss much more about wanting to ensure that management and shareholders are aligned for the long haul. If management is focused too much on short-term results, long-term investors will be hurt.

Years ago, John Sculley took over from Steve Jobs as CEO of Apple, and he started raising the prices of Apple computers. Initially, profitability was terrific, but then the company lost market share. The same thing happened with Lou Gerstner at American Express when he instituted a pricing structure that made Amex more expensive than Visa or Mastercard. Soon enough, businesses stopped accepting American Express cards.

You can absolutely boost prices in the short term when you have loyal customers, but you may wind up costing a company lots of value over a long period of time. This is why management incentives are so important.

Related to this is a point about price elasticity. Elasticity can vary across markets and time. One of Warren Buffett's key insights into investing in Coca-Cola and other consumer brands is that customers are fairly price-insensitive for products that are seen to be far superior to the competition or have particularly loyal customer bases. Price increases may not reduce demand, which is what Lou Gerstner hoped would happen with Amex, but he turned out to be wrong. Today, cereal and other consumer brands face more elastic demand due to an increase in high-quality private alternatives, the ease of online commerce, and the fact that, in some cases, the price lever has already been pulled to its maximum effect, and even loyal customers will eventually reach a limit.

International Considerations

Finally, it is worth paying attention to where on the globe a business is based in trying to determine its value. The emerging markets are interesting both as a potential place to invest as well as a setting that can allow fundamental analysis to prove its worth. The United States currently comprises over 58 percent of world market capitalization, even while containing only 4 percent of the world's population and less than 25 percent of global GDP (roughly 15 percent on a purchasing power parity basis). Market capitalization in the US is growing increasingly concentrated among the largest companies. Apple alone is worth more than the combined value of the Russell 2000 index, which tracks the companies in the United States ranked 1000th through 3000th by size. Apple and Microsoft together make up nearly 14 percent of the value of the S&P 500.[10]

The total US market capitalization relative to GDP is one of the highest in the world, and, in fact, nine of the top ten market capitalizations are in countries where the birth rate is not sufficient to sustain the population. On the other hand, many countries in the emerging markets have relatively young populations. These countries are in need of enormous amounts of capital if they are to develop successfully. The developed countries are seeing significant political pushback against immigration, limiting population growth since the birth rate is low. This provides an opening, if not a requirement, for emerging markets to step up.

The emerging markets need to create efficient capital markets, improve corporate governance, and improve accounting standards in order to finance the corporate growth that is needed to employ their populations—and as they do this, opportunities for investment will expand. It is in the interest of the developed countries to help the developing countries improve these features, in service of their own future business prospects. Companies in emerging markets trade at a significant discount right now compared to the developed world, but that merely indicates potential for greater returns going forward.

Right alongside the pure demographic issue of population growth driving growth in the emerging markets is that the distribution of patents and intellectual property is changing rapidly. The United States used to dominate the world in terms of patents and intellectual property, but rising education in the emerging markets is changing things. People with graduate degrees are responsible for roughly 70 percent of patents filed.[11] The emerging markets are growing rapidly as far as the percentage of all people in the world with graduate degrees. More foreign-born residents of the United States have graduate degrees than native-born citizens.[12] Intellectual property is shifting in that direction, from the developed markets to the emerging markets.

Driven by the same trends toward greater education, the middle class is growing rapidly in emerging markets. With middle-class growth will come the demand for more democracy and for the continued liberalization of economic markets. Korea and Taiwan have illustrated this path, and others will follow. With the growth of the middle class, the demand for more education will continue to increase, propelling further growth.

The growth of the middle class as a percentage of the total population of a sample of emerging markets can be found in the graph that follows.[13]

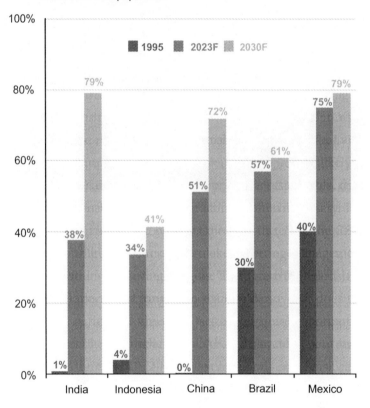

Growth of the middle class
Percent of total population

- ■ 1995 ■ 2023F ■ 2030F

India: 1% / 38% / 79%
Indonesia: 4% / 34% / 41%
China: 0% / 51% / 72%
Brazil: 30% / 57% / 61%
Mexico: 40% / 75% / 79%

Indeed, the result, as illustrated in the diagram that follows, courtesy of Bloomberg, is that emerging markets continue to trade at a discount, showing that there is tremendous opportunity for smart investment.[14]

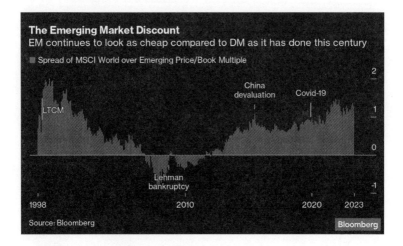

These factors discussed in this chapter are all critical in evaluating businesses from a distance. When you get closer, you can look at the management team and governance decisions, which are worth an examination in the next chapter.

CHAPTER 4
GOVERNANCE

Governance is an exceptionally important topic to cover. A well-governed company makes a far better investment opportunity than a poorly governed one; a company's board structure and management decisions are so important to evaluate when considering investments. In this chapter, we can start by looking at management and its incentives and decision-making, then move to looking at board structures and other governance considerations.

Management

Evaluating the quality of a company's management is critical when deciding whether to invest—but it is also very difficult. Fundamentally, the most important thing to look for is alignment: Are the interests of management aligned with the interests of investors? Later in this chapter, we will discuss specific ways in which alignment can be evaluated and supported, particularly around share ownership and compensation. But first, it is helpful to look at what makes a good manager in the first place, and what we should be searching for when we evaluate management.

We often evaluate performance in hindsight: if a company did well, we give credit to the management team; if the company did poorly, we blame management's decisions. This unquestionably overweighs the influence of management (success and failure are often far more significantly governed by external events largely out of management's control), and it also assumes that what happened in the past is fully indicative of what will happen in the future. There are ways to assess management quality in hindsight, but the challenge for an investor is predicting who will be effective going forward.

Effective Management Qualities

It would be easy if there existed a set of manager qualities that were effective for every organization at every point in time, and, even better, if those qualities were easily ascertained. Unfortunately, on both counts, there is not all that much of solid value to offer. But there are a few ideas worth exploring. First, there has been some interesting research on management personality types and traits, and even some that is data-dependent rather than merely subjective.

One academic study, "Which CEO Characteristics and Abilities Matter?," examined CEO candidates at companies involved in leveraged buyout and venture capital transactions, assessing these candidates in terms of a range of personal skills and attributes based on four-hour structured interviews and looking at data about their education and employment history.[1] The study found a correlation between certain execution-related measures ("efficient," "organized," "detailed," "follows through," "persistent," "proactive," "sets high standards," and "holds people accountable") and success, with no advantage for incumbent CEOs as opposed to newcomers, when other traits were held constant. Interestingly, the authors found a negative correlation between success and what they described as team-related skills ("teamwork," "listening skills," "open to criticism," and "treats people with respect"). (The authors do note a limitation with the study, as it focused specifically on buyout and VC-funded companies. "As a result," the authors write, "it is not possible to know whether the results generalize to CEOs of other firms, particularly public companies."[2])

A second study, "CEO Personality and Firm Policies," sought to analyze CEO personality in terms of agreeableness, conscientiousness, extraversion, neuroticism, and openness to experience.[3] The study found that conscientiousness—having a cautious temperament—was negatively associated with growth, and extraversion was negatively associated with both contemporaneous and future return on assets and cash flows. The authors do counsel that these relationships may not be causal, but they still leave the reader with something to think about.

In Geoff Smart and Randy Street's book *Who*, a *New York Times* bestseller built on more than thirteen hundred interviews with over twenty billionaires and three hundred CEOs, the findings track the other studies just mentioned.[4] Respect, teamwork, listening skills, and being open to criticism, while desirable characteristics generally, are not effective in generating economic success. The critical competencies, the authors found, are moving quickly, acting aggressively, working hard, demonstrating persistence, and holding people accountable to high standards. This profile type, which the authors called the "cheetah," generated value 100 percent of the time.[5]

On the other hand, it is worth noting that narcissists do not make good managers. The "soft skills" may not drive economic success, but narcissistic leaders who undermine collaboration and create a toxic work environment need to be rooted out.[6]

It is also important not to conflate the CEO and the company. A management team is more than one individual, and credit or blame usually doesn't fall on one person given how complex most companies and operating environments are. There are times the CEO is hugely impactful—M&A decisions, for instance—but there are also times when you miss real insight if you only look at the top leader and not the other executives.

The challenge is that even if you identify the characteristics you are looking for in a management team, it is not always easy to figure out which managers have them, and which managers don't—especially in situations where you, as an investor, don't get to subject someone to your own four-hour structured interview. While some personality work has been done by analyzing word choice from publicly available documents—there is some interesting work on this front in James Pennebaker's *The Secret Life of Pronouns*, which discusses how you can use word choice to identify personal traits as well as to determine whether someone is telling the truth—it is hard enough to gain useful insight from in-person meetings, so I would be wary of presuming you can gain larger psychological insights from your own analysis of the precise language in the company's materials than the conclusions that are clearly apparent.[7]

Management Interviews

In situations where you do get to interview a management team yourself, there are benefits to be gained, but what to ask isn't always clear. There may be questions that one can ask in an interview that would determine management quality, but, for the most part, I never discovered them. I certainly met with many management teams that sounded terrific in meetings but subsequently turned out to be disastrous. Others were not so impressive in meetings but were revealed to be excellent.

The problem is that the answers managers give aren't always honest. At least in the US, very specific questions regarding the potential for mergers, spinoffs, or earnings prospects are unlikely to be answered honestly. Some of these questions might yield useful (honest) answers overseas, but US management teams, in particular, have generally been well-coached to not disclose material nonpublic information. The nonanswers that management teams give to many specific material questions can, in fact, be misleading. Other specific questions may lead management to give answers that they believe the questioner wants to hear. The truth is that management often rises to top positions based on their presentation ability or other personal attributes that may have nothing to do with the ability to successfully manage a large company. Investment bankers and other specialized firms exist to counsel management teams on what investors want to hear; it is therefore not surprising that investors can be misled by excellent management presentations.

In interviewing management teams, the most informative approach is to ask open-ended questions, such as "What are you focused on?" or "What are your key objectives and goals?" Over time, I did find one particularly worthwhile question, which we will come back to a bit later in the chapter, regarding capital allocation. Warren Buffett, in particular, has talked about the importance of capital allocation when it comes to great managers. "I think you judge management by two yardsticks," Buffett said. "One is how well they run the business, and I think you can learn a lot about that by reading about both what they've accomplished and what their competitors have accomplished and seeing how they have allocated capital over time. [The other measure is how they treat their shareholders.]"[8]

If given the opportunity, it is always a good idea to ask management teams how they make decisions regarding capital allocation—and to ask in an open and nonjudgmental way. It is remarkable the range of answers that you end up receiving, and those answers may tell you a lot about how the team will perform. In hindsight, another benefit of management interviews was allowing me to identify which management teams actually followed through on what they promised. If taking a long-term approach to your investing, you can look at management teams over time and gain insight into which ones actually do what they say.

Evaluating Management Performance

The reality is that great managers do not exist independent of the context in which they need to manage. Different situations call for different skills and talents, and sometimes even the greatest management team needs to change if a business needs to turn around. Existing management, no matter its past success, often has a difficult time turning around a business or making a major transition. Managers are ultimately human, with the same biases as anyone else. It is very hard for anyone to dismantle a business that he has built, to fire long-term colleagues, and to completely change how things are run. It is difficult to cannibalize existing businesses when technology or demand shifts in some way that requires an entirely new approach. If a company is floundering and needs real change, it probably needs a new CEO from outside the business and possibly from outside the industry. The company may even be an excellent candidate for a private equity takeover. Private equity ownership may allow for changes that would be difficult for existing management to undertake or, even more broadly, for a company to undertake while it is public. Low-performing companies that promote from within are asking to remain low-performing.

The arc of time has shown me that people don't change much—and this certainly applies to management teams. A great clue as to how management will behave in the future is how they have behaved in the past. To think about this from one angle, leopards don't change their spots. Managers frequently use the same playbook, even when things turn out poorly (leading to recurrent bankruptcies and even worse—see, for instance, the case of Barry Minkow, founder of the $100 million Ponzi scheme ZZZZ Best, who, after serving time in prison, ended up defrauding his church and landing back in prison[9]). Whether repeating the same mistakes at one organization or moving to a new company, it is hard to change strategy.

At the same time, it is hard to effect change at many companies; businesses want to go on running themselves in whatever way they have been run for years, and perhaps decades, and they're very resistant to change, even when the need is pretty obvious. Credit Suisse is an example of a company that resisted change for far too long and ended up collapsing. They were plagued with scandal after scandal, yet they did not clean house. Senior managers clearly needed to be fired and replaced with people with a new set of ethics, yet it didn't happen, and the business failed.[10]

Having been acquired in 2023 by UBS, Credit Suisse will hopefully clean itself up, but this could have happened sooner with a change of management. The bank could have stayed as an independent company and been successful over time: it wasn't that the business was inherently bad, but existing leadership didn't want to change and didn't recognize that a change needed to happen.

To effectively analyze management, you must first determine what kind of leader the company needs at the present time. Cost-cutters will try to cut costs. Growth managers will try to grow. People are prisoners of their pasts. They want to do what they know. Managers are often biased toward the businesses that they grew up in. Does the company need the skills that the manager has demonstrated in past roles? Someone with a background in sales and marketing may not be the best choice for a company that has a manufacturing problem. Bringing a cost-cutter into a lean organization may not yield significant results, while bringing the same individual into a fat organization might be exactly what is needed. There have been "savior" CEOs in many situations who come in to turn things around, but this can lead to short-term outperformance and longer-term underperformance since the incentive is to show progress quickly.

How do you figure out what the organization needs? Businesses are like any other kind of organism. They learn to exist in a particular environment. When profitability is high and growth is plentiful, organizations tend to become sloppy and fat—it's only natural. Companies in industries where the technology or end demand has fundamentally changed often need drastic fundamental change themselves. Companies with very low margins in hypercompetitive businesses may need a fundamental rethink of their mission.

This is hard to pull off, and most managers are reluctant to undertake big pivots because of the short-term effect on stock price and the uncertainty of success overall. I will share two examples of companies that did manage to increase focus on their core, high-margin businesses while exiting other businesses. The results in both cases were dramatic.

The first example is Texas Instruments (TI). In 1997, TI off-loaded its defense electronics business to Raytheon for $2.95 billion in cash. The deal was for as much as $1 billion more than initially expected and meant that both companies were able to increase their focus on core operations. Raytheon was looking to increase its military business, and TI used the deal to help concentrate the company around its computer chip business. As the *New York Times* wrote at the time, "For Texas Instruments, based in Dallas, the sale would help it concentrate on making computer chips, another business where size and financial strength matter because of the huge costs of research, development and plant construction."[11]

TI's stock price doubled from around $8 per share when the deal was announced to $16 per share by September of 1997. But it dipped by the end of the year and lingered in the midteens throughout the first part of 1998. In June of 1998, the company announced another transaction. The industry-focused *EE Times* wrote on June 18, 1998, "After months of speculation and growing losses, Texas Instruments announced Thursday that it was pulling out of dynamic RAM (DRAM) devices by selling the memory business to Micron Technology . . . . 'Several years ago, TI set a course to become a company focused on its leadership position in digital signal processing solutions,' said Thomas J. Engibous, TI chairman, CEO, and president. 'With this latest transaction, TI truly becomes a DSP solutions company . . .'"[12]

The result of TI's further focus on its core business was dramatic success. The stock price began a steep rise for nearly two years that peaked at $91 per share in March of 2000, and as of this writing, the stock trades at more than $165 per share.

Another example is Verisign. The internet infrastructure firm spent from 2007 to 2010 unloading more than a dozen business units for an estimated $2 billion in the spirit of generating cash and focusing on its infrastructure and security strengths. The company sold off its insurance business, consulting business, messaging business, and more between 2007 and 2009[13] before then selling its $1.28 billion authentication business to Symantec.[14]

Initial predictions for Verisign were bleak. One analyst, Jon Oltsik, writing for security and risk management publication *CSO*, said at the time, "Verisign's divestment is just the latest sad chapter for a company that once had a market cap in the tens of billions of dollars. . . . It's worth examining the troubled history of Verisign as a case study of what not to do."[15] From a stock price hovering around $25 per share in 2010, Verisign now trades at more than $185 per share a little more than a dozen years later.

Management Decision-Making

Despite the challenges of figuring out if a manager or management team has what it takes to lead a company to success, there is still plenty of evidence you can turn to in order to analyze how management approaches the job and figure out whether they are doing all that is possible to lead the company in the right direction. Fundamentally, you want to look at whether there is a system underlying the decisions management is making, and then you want to look very closely at the big question mentioned in the previous section: How is management allocating capital, and does this allocation align with the interests of a long-term shareholder?

A key question for companies is about management systems and controls. Some companies make a point of highlighting their superior management systems, crediting them for much of their success. The global science and technology innovator Danaher is an example here, specifically their Danaher Business System. As the company writes, "Success at Danaher doesn't happen by accident. We have a proven system for achieving it. We call it the Danaher Business System (DBS), and it drives every aspect of our culture and performance. We use DBS to guide what we do, measure how well we execute, and create options for doing even better—including improving DBS itself."[16]

In essence, the DBS—"exceptional *PEOPLE* develop outstanding *PLANS* and execute them using world-class tools to construct sustainable *PROCESSES*, resulting in superior *PERFORMANCE*," as they put it—is just one formulation among many. These systems typically end up with organizations driven by key performance indicators (KPIs) that can involve all areas of the business. Companies that employ these types of systems seem to experience better results that are backed up by data. Companies that use KPIs are more efficient.[17] The World Management Survey—looking at management practices at firms around the world—has indeed found that "higher management scores are positively and significantly associated with higher productivity, firm size, profitability, sales growth, market value, and survival"[18] and that on a macroeconomic level, better management can explain a quarter of the total productivity gap between the US and other countries.

The rationale is fairly straightforward: better management systems allow companies to better track their progress toward goals and lead to more knowledge for the management team about the current state of affairs. If management knows what is going on in the business, it is able to more quickly and more effectively react to changed circumstances. It may also be the case that better management systems can lead to companies being able to report earlier following the end of a quarter, helping internal audiences stay on target and allowing external audiences better visibility into the business.

For more about business systems, an excellent book to consult is John Doerr's *Measure What Matters*, which highlights the systems used by some of America's most successful companies.[19]

Capital Allocation

As mentioned previously, one of the most important decisions that CEOs have to make is how to allocate capital. Capital allocation is a tremendous driver of shareholder value. The menu of options is standard—dividends, share repurchases, reinvestment in the business, and acquisitions (mergers). But the way companies decide is all over the map.

Many companies have a dividend and exhibit a desire to grow this dividend at a steady rate. This is taken as accepted wisdom when it's not clear that it should be. To the extent that there's an argument to make for it, one can say that it probably indicates a level of stability in the business, and stability is one way to protect against job loss for the managers at the top. So the wisdom around dividend growth would seem to be motivated by self-preservation more than service to shareholders.

Share repurchases are often viewed favorably by investors, yet they typically yield unsatisfactory results for long-term shareholders. Research has found that share repurchases actually have a negligible effect on share prices in the short term and do not meaningfully affect future cash flow.[20] The reason they don't yield long-term results is fairly obvious when the math is carefully considered. Management often repurchases shares when a company is experiencing very strong cash flow. Yet strong cash flow typically occurs when the share price is elevated or perhaps even overvalued. Repurchasing an overvalued stock is pretty clearly destructive in terms of long-term shareholder value. Ideally, you would like the management of a company with an overvalued stock to be issuing shares instead. (If they have excess cash, they could pay a special dividend.)

Not all share repurchase strategies are the same. The cable company Charter Communications took advantage of cheap debt to consistently repurchase Charter shares. Comcast, essentially in the same business, pursued a capital allocation strategy less focused on share repurchase. Partially as a result of these different allocation strategies, Charter's sales per share grew by 15.6 percent over the decade ending in 2023, while Comcast grew at 9.1 percent. Capital allocation and share repurchase strategies are just one component of a company's broader set of financial and operating opportunities and risks. For example, Altice USA—also in the same business—pursued a strategy focused on share repurchases but has had much worse cumulative returns for long-term shareholders when compared to its peers.

Management teams that behave rationally (and there are vanishingly few that always do) should always be evaluating their own share price and determining whether they believe the stock is undervalued or overvalued. As managers of the company, they are in possession of far more information to determine this than the shareholders have. Yet it is fascinating how few management teams attempt to objectively establish what their company is worth. Most are on a never-ending quest to try to raise the share price. When the stock is undervalued, it may make sense to re purchase shares (depending on other potential uses of funds for mergers or internal projects); of course, often when the stock is undervalued, there are cash flow issues or other obstacles to repurchasing shares. There may be fundamental issues that the market is worried about, such as a recession, or new competitive challenges for the company. Managements are often loath to borrow in order to repurchase undervalued shares, although this can, in fact, be a perfectly rational decision.

An example to look at is Brighthouse Financial. The company repurchased a substantial number of shares in 2020, after the downturn that occurred in response to the COVID-19 pandemic. This was a risky move—uncertainty was high—but management saw an opportunity to repurchase shares at a sizable discount and decided to make the move. This decision led to Brighthouse Financial substantially outperforming the S&P 500 over the two years that followed.

When it comes to reinvestment in the business (internal projects), management approaches are all over the map. Some companies allow individual divisions to reinvest the cash that they are able to generate. Some allocate capital based on what is needed to stay competitive in the various lines of business. Others try to maintain employment whenever possible. Some have a formulaic approach to allocating capital with each division getting a certain percentage of the available cash for investment. No matter the specifics of the approach, you want to look for a management team that has a very deliberate and analytical process for trying to determine where the highest returns will be generated and a system for effectively allocating capital to those highest-return projects.

Mergers

Finally, there are mergers. On average, mergers are value-destructive for shareholders even when there are incentives for managers to seek them. There is an excellent book about mergers by Robert F. Bruner, titled *Deals from Hell: M&A Lessons That Rise above the Ashes*.[21] The book looks at twelve failed mergers, and why they failed. "It's common knowledge that about half of all merger and acquisition (M&A) transactions destroy value for the buyer's shareholders," explains the publisher, "and about three-quarters fall short of the expectations prevailing at the time the deal is announced."

In my experience, it is fairly easy to determine whether or not a merger has any chance of success in terms of adding to long-term shareholder value. The best mergers tend to be small, bolt-on acquisitions where the acquiring company can provide superior distribution, additional technology, greater scale in manufacturing or advertising, or some other kind of easily articulated, tangible benefit to the acquired organization. There is also a benefit to taking out competitors, to the extent allowed by regulators. However, there is often a problem with large, so-called "strategic" mergers where there is no clear benefit or synergy from the combination of the two businesses. If the benefits are not readily obvious, they probably don't exist. There is also tremendous integration risk with mergers. Bringing a small organization into a large organization carries real risk that innovation or esprit de corps can be crushed. Combining two large organizations together means eliminating large numbers of managers, eliminating duplicate systems, and merging cultures and accounting. These factors can absolutely sink an otherwise positive merger.

One example to look at is the merger of Union Pacific and Southern Pacific. In the summer of 1996, the US government approved the merger of Union Pacific and Southern Pacific railroads, making Union Pacific (the surviving company) the largest rail company in the United States, covering thirty-one thousand miles in twenty-four states and running two thousand trains each day.[22] "The combinations are just devastating," one Southern Pacific official told the *Washington Post* at the time.[23] "You can knock hours off some routes. Strategically, it's a superb merger." While the merger made a great deal of economic sense, integration issues made the deal look like a catastrophe at first.

"For nearly a year, freight train service west of the Mississippi River has been all but derailed by the merger of the Union Pacific and Southern Pacific railroads," wrote *Fortune* in 1998.[24] "Billions of dollars worth of freight shipments, supposed to arrive in three or four days, have been taking thirty days, forty-five days. Sometimes they get lost. For months, UP has been losing dozens of tank cars belonging to Olin Corp. How does a railroad lose tank cars? Who knows?"

The *Wall Street Journal* added, "[UP's] railroad safety record, marred by three fatal crashes in three months, is being characterized as a 'fundamental breakdown' by federal regulators. Its route system west of the Mississippi River has slipped into near gridlock in many places, with thousands of freight cars backed up in the Houston area alone."[25]

But then, the tide turned. A 2004 analysis by Dennis Breen of the Federal Trade Commission's Bureau of Economics found that most of the expected postmerger benefits were, in fact, realized, with an estimated $829 million of value created by 2001.[26]"Consistent with the merger-related operating plan, [benefits] include shorter routes, directional running, reduced interchange of cars between railroads, enhanced car utilization . . . combined freight yards and freight car shops, and combined offices and computer systems," wrote Breen. This was in addition to labor cost savings, savings from combining headquarters, and more.

Union Pacific's stock price was around $11 per share when the merger was announced. As I write this, it sits at more than $230 per share, an astonishing rise.

The problem with expecting all mergers to turn out as well as Union Pacific's eventually did is that management often has interests related to mergers that diverge substantially from those of the long-term shareholders. Incentives are discussed more generally later in this chapter, but managers have to prefer stability, as it serves as insurance that they won't be replaced. Managers would also generally prefer to run larger organizations. One reason is that they can justify higher levels of compensation if the organization is bigger. Management often claims a desire to diversify the business. This does provide greater stability, and as a shareholder it is absolutely the case that you don't want the business to go into financial distress—but you, as an investor, are fully capable of diversifying risk on your own with other holdings. You don't need a company to merge in order to accomplish the same thing for your portfolio. And your own diversification doesn't introduce downside to the business like a merger can. The potential loss from having a conglomerate business is that there is less focus and more complexity, both of which can work against the interests of the long-term shareholder. It is rare, ultimately, that conglomerates sell for more than the sum of their parts, especially if the businesses are different, separable, and provide no synergies to each other.

I should note that there is also a strong set of incentives for management to not sell their company, even if there would be a business interest in pursuing the acquisition. One of the easiest ways for managers to find themselves out of a job is to sell the company. Often companies that are put up for sale have CEOs that are nearing retirement. Similarly, companies are reluctant to divest businesses or shut down significant divisions, even if it makes economic sense to do so. Managers do not want their businesses to get smaller.

There is a particular risk when it comes to mergers paid for by stock. Historical research has shown that the shareholders of acquiring companies fare worse in stock transactions than they do in transactions paid for with cash.[27] I think this makes good sense. Cash is a very real thing from a manager's perspective, and in the case of cash acquired by taking on debt, it must be paid back. Shares, on the other hand, feel like free money to many managers. Of course, for the long-term investor, this is not the case. Investors need to remain focused on per-share numbers. Mergers paid for in shares can be very expensive to the long-term shareholder, especially if they don't yield the necessary synergy.

As a practical guide for evaluating mergers, I propose a fairly detailed series of questions that investors should ask across five categories of inquiry:

PRICE

- What is the premium paid over the predeal stock price?
- What is the valuation of the company being acquired?
- How big is the company being acquired relative to the acquirer? (Bigger acquisitions are more dangerous, but even small acquisitions can send a message regarding the mentality of management.)
- Is the price in cash or stock? How much dilution will occur? Did the acquirer need to borrow money? Is there a bond idea here? (As noted previously, the use of cash seems to indicate that the merger is more likely to be successful for the acquirer's shareholders.)
- How did the acquirer's stock react to news of the deal? (This can provide some indication of the future performance of the acquirer's stock once and if the deal is concluded.)

BUSINESS RATIONALE

- Are the companies in the same line of business?
- Are there any synergies from the merger? (Think in terms of shared distribution, R&D, manufacturing, and systems.)
- Was the merger done out of desperation or to prevent an acquisition by a competitor?
- How strategic (read: potentially bad for shareholders) was the rationale for the acquisition versus how opportunistic (read: they hope to make money)?
- Were the assets identified through proprietary work or through an auction? (Assets that are sole-sourced tend to be better assets.)
- Does the acquirer understand the line of business being acquired?
- Does the acquisition appear well-planned? Does the acquirer appear to know what it bought?
- Who has accountability over the acquired assets? (Assets where business leads, rather than corporate development teams, have accountability tend to work out better because corporate development teams are often compensated based on deal flow rather than quality.)
- Are asset sales part of the plan? How reasonable are the assumptions regarding those assets? How sensitive is the deal to realizations from asset sales that are below the plan? Could the company be placed in financial distress if the asset sales are not completed quickly?

CULTURAL DIFFERENCES

- How closely do the cultures align? (You do not want an immediate us-versus-them situation to develop. A hypercompetitive sales-driven organization, for instance, will probably not fit well with a conservative, process-driven company. Lots of people may leave, and those who don't may be unhappy.)
- Is there a cross-border element to the merger? Can people from both nationalities achieve positions of responsibility, or is the organization nationalistic?

CONTROL

- Is there a clear CEO and CFO? (Be extremely suspicious of power-sharing deals in which there is not.)
- Is there one defined headquarters? (Be extremely suspicious of dual-headquarters situations.)
- Are systems and finance staffs being consolidated? (Be extremely suspicious of reasons for not consolidating these elements.)

SPEED OF INTEGRATION

- Has the acquirer made comparable acquisitions in the past, and did they work out?
- Are they trying to extract too much too fast in terms of synergies? (Sometimes this is driven by paying too

much for the deal.)

- What is the initial plan of integration and the time-table for it? Is it being followed? Is the integration working? What is happening to customer service and satisfaction? What is the planned attrition? Are people leaving who the company should not want to leave?

In sum, be very suspicious of Wall Street research regarding a merger. Mergers pay a lot of people's salaries, and the resulting asset sales and securities issues can create tremendous profit opportunities for the bankers and brokers. The incentives are clearly to write glowing reports in support of the deal. More broadly, the ideal answer when it comes to capital allocation is that management should have a careful system in place to evaluate alternatives. You want to know that potential mergers, internal investments, and share repurchases are being considered using an internal rate of return or net-present-value framework and that dividends are being paid only when none of the alternatives offers an adequate return. Of course, this is rarely the answer in reality, evidenced by the general lack of special dividends. Companies rarely return cash to the shareholders, yet there are times when this is exactly what you would want them to do. Cash flow is not constant. Divestitures and other one-off events can supply the company with large amounts of available funds. These should be returned to shareholders when no better option exists.

Aligning Incentives

The merger discussion brings up a larger point when it comes to evaluating management. Incentives are not always aligned, and I believe the best companies—when looking at where to put your investment dollars—will do whatever they can to improve that alignment. To examine alignment, we can look at management share ownership, and then we can also look more broadly at compensation structure and the kind of compensation incentives that are most ideal for driving strong alignment of incentives.

The obvious starting point: Large shareholdings by management clearly align management interests with the long-term shareholder. It is very much worth examining the size of shareholdings relative to management compensation. When shareholdings are small as a percentage of overall compensation, keeping their jobs may become the primary focus of management as opposed to looking at long-term shareholder value.

It is also worth looking at whether management is actively purchasing or selling shares. Many management teams are compensated with stock options. Are these options being held to maturity? In the absence of inside information, holding options to maturity is the value-maximizing strategy. Early exercise of options followed by the sale of the received shares is a warning sign that things may be awry.

Generally, management teams will sell stock on an ongoing basis. This is understandable behavior in the absence of inside information. The options are often a substantial part of their income, and it is fair for them to sell some of their holdings. Taxes must be paid on gains for the exercise of options, so cash is needed. When management abruptly stops selling, this can sometimes be a sign of better things to come for the stock price.

Management purchases of stock are much rarer than sales. Large purchases are especially rare. But these signals can be manipulated. Management teams recognize that some shareholders pay close attention to insider purchases and sales of stock. They will often deliberately purchase significant shares when the company is under pressure as a signal that they have confidence in the company. But it may be a false signal.

Some companies require officers and directors to own a certain number of shares of stock, often related to their position and level of compensation. This can also be a misleading signal. Management can create planned sales programs in order to avoid accusations of benefiting from insider trading. Again, a misleading signal at times. The *Wall Street Journal* points out that these planned sale programs are often timed well in terms of disposing of the company's stock.[28] These programs can be manipulated, as explained in a 2021 Stanford article, "Gaming the System: Three 'Red Flags' of Potential 10b5-1 Abuse."[29] The article finds that "a subset of executives use 10b5-1 plans to engage in opportunistic, large-scale selling of company shares." The manipulation relies on three characteristics of these plans: plans with a short cooling-off period; plans that entail only a single trade; and plans adopted in a given quarter that begin trading before that quarter's earnings announcement. "Sales made pursuant to these plans avoid significant losses and foreshadow considerable stock price declines that are well in excess of industry peers," write the authors.

Even without purposeful manipulation, we see some managers justify selling stock by saying that they want to prudently diversify their holdings. These managers ignore Andrew Carnegie's famous saying, "The way to become rich is to put all your eggs in one basket and then watch that basket."[30]

The structure of management compensation more broadly is a topic that is often overlooked. Many companies incentivize management teams on factors that are not in any way related to value creation for long-term shareholders. Some companies now incentivize on various ESG factors, especially in Europe. Some compensation structures yield incentives to boost short-term performance, but at terrible cost to the long-term shareholder—for instance, cutting deep into R&D and new product development, raising prices on products (resulting in lost market share), channel stuffing (where excessive amounts of product are sent to distribution channels), providing financing for a product on less-than-commercially reasonable terms, or, an old favorite, accounting changes.

Each of these approaches can result in near-term boosts to profits, but at long-term peril.

The CEO of Fruit of the Loom, Bill Farley, for instance, was the highest-paid executive in Chicago in 1997 and was out of a job by 1999, the company having lost $576 million and filing for bankruptcy.[31] (Farley later settled a class action suit where he was accused of fraud and insider trading.[32])

The academic literature on executive compensation shows that compensation packages do help align manager and shareholder interests.[33] Executive compensation is positively related to share price performance, managers choose to structure accounting processes in ways that increase their bonuses, new compensation plans for executives are linked to higher share prices, and managers make fewer merger bids that may lower stock prices when they hold more stock in their firms.

Kevin Murphy of the University of Southern California has written extensively about executive compensation issues. "Stock-based incentives are important drivers of managerial actions and corporate performance," Murphy believes, but he also acknowledges that "there remains little direct evidence . . . on the returns a company can expect from introducing aggressive performance-based compensation plans."[34]

The problem, according to one paper, "CEO Bonus Plans: And How to Fix Them," is that "almost all CEO and executive bonus plans have serious design flaws that limit their benefits dramatically. Such poorly designed executive bonus plans destroy value by providing incentives to manipulate the timing of earnings, mislead the board about organizational capabilities, take on excessive (or insufficient) risk, forgo profitable projects, and ignore the cost of capital."[35]

David Larcker, the director of the Corporate Governance Research Initiative at Stanford Graduate School of Business, has written about how private equity companies are often successful at generating large returns—and, as it happens, executive compensation in private equity is more heavily weighted toward equity.[36] The heavy use of equity compensation may well be serving to better align interests and is data that public boards should consider when developing compensation plans.

It is interesting to see—and note this in the following graph[37]—that the US has the highest share of stock and options as a percentage of compensation when compared with other nations. Options are widely issued in technology companies in particular, and perhaps this is part of the reason why the US is home to most of the world's leading technology companies. The people and governments in many other countries have a far greater objection to wide disparities in income than we see in the US. This is why salaries rather than bonuses or stock grants form a greater proportion of CEO compensation in other countries. This idea also connects with the fact that US companies have a notably greater ability to remain effective when run by professional management as opposed to the company's founders or a founding family. Foreign companies run without active family ownership often suffer from lax accountability between shareholders and management. Looking at the graph, it is interesting to see that the UK, Ireland, and Switzerland have the next-highest levels of stock and option compensation. The UK and Ireland are more committed to free markets than most nations. Switzerland is unique in having a very high level of equity relative to the size of its economy. Some of this may result from Switzerland having more shareholder-friendly policies than other countries.

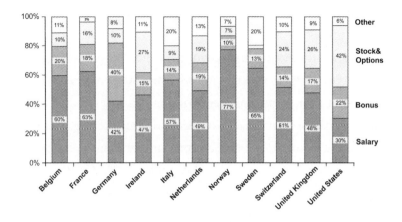

I have noticed over time the prevalence of incentives based on gross sales or earnings. But the long-term shareholder needs to care about revenues and earnings *per share*. This is a critical difference. Management benefits from running a larger company, as discussed earlier—more compensation, more prestige—but investors benefit from an increased share price, not merely increased revenue. We need to look for compensation packages that reward decisions that permanently propel the share price upward. Restricted stock can be a powerful tool in this regard, as well as a focus on long-term incentives rather than measures that can be manipulated in the short run.

Research has shown that the most favored mechanism for resolving the problem of shareholder misalignment is having concentrated control in the hands of large shareholders.[38] Even though there are potential downsides here when it comes to possible collusion between large shareholders and management, as well as reduced liquidity, concentrated control does prove to help mitigate misalignment and solve collective action issues.

It should be noted that changes in incentives can presage changes to business strategy. Microsemi CEO James Peterson's decision to forgo multiple years of bonuses in exchange for a one-time share grant created a situation where, if triggers were hit, Peterson's payday could be comparable to his cumulative compensation over his prior *seventeen years* as CEO. Almost surely not coincidentally, the company agreed to be sold to its competitor, Microchip, during the period in question. Almost surely not coincidentally as well, Microchip soon found that Microsemi had "stuffed its sales channel with inventory to inflate its revenue figures," according to *Investor's Business Daily*, leaving Microchip with a "mess."[39] Changed incentives should lead to extra scrutiny when big corporate decisions soon follow.

It should also be noted that not all stock options are created equal. Many companies issue restricted stock units (RSUs) rather than traditional stock options. RSUs provide you with the stock itself at the end of the vesting period rather than just an option to buy. This can change incentives. Bill Gurley, a general partner at the Silicon Valley venture capital firm Benchmark, has criticized RSUs for failing to align incentives. "RSU reality," he posted on Twitter (now X), "95%+ of RSUs are sold on vest date. Ask any public CFO. They are not an 'ownership in the business' vehicle. They are a cash-like payment hidden in a construct companies hope you will 'ignore.'"[40]

Boards of Directors

So much of what we look to analyze about management is, in fact, controlled by the board. Directors set compensation plans and thus have the power to shape management incentives, and directors approve or reject mergers, which, as discussed, are often not in the best interest of long-term shareholders. An analysis of management must take into account the board as well.

There is a surprising amount of variation when it comes to boards of directors. Boards vary in size, composition of membership, and share ownership. There is some academic evidence that smaller boards are better, with multiple studies showing an inverse relationship between board size and firm value.[41, 42] (Other studies find no relationship.[43]) This makes intuitive sense. Large groups are prone to inertia. A large group of people is unlikely to take any kind of decisive action: if everyone is responsible, then no one is responsible. And decisive action is often necessary. The most important job of the board of directors is to fire the CEO, when appropriate. Other crucial roles are setting management compensation and approving mergers. These are critical decisions from the perspective of long-term shareholders.

In my experience, former CEOs are often quite important to have on a board, and I believe every board should have at least one current or former CEO. The person who will most easily and quickly recognize when a company's CEO is not performing well is almost certainly going to be another CEO. Research shows that there is a positive stock price reaction to the first outside CEO being appointed to a board, although no further effect when subsequent CEOs are appointed.[44] Boards often include academics, lawyers, accountants, investment bankers, or other community leaders. Having never run corporations, these individuals are not likely to recognize when the CEO is floundering and are not accustomed to making big decisions. They are also ill-prepared to step into interim CEO roles if necessary during transitions, as well as ill-equipped to identify the right CEO to lead the company next. Research, in fact, shows that financial experts on a board—commercial bankers and investment bankers, specifically—do influence corporate decisions, but not in ways that ultimately benefit shareholders.[45]

"Investment bankers on boards are associated with larger bond issues but worse acquisitions," write the authors of "Financial Expertise of Directors" in the *Journal of Financial Economics*.[46] On the other hand, there is some evidence that board members with a finance background do reduce the likelihood of fraudulent financials.

The past history of directors can, of course, be instructive regarding the future performance of these same directors. Directors who have a poor history of performance will often have a future history of poor performance. Very high levels of cash compensation for directors, unsurprisingly, can be indicative of the directors' likelihood to lack interest in challenging management. In the worst cases, directors might be chosen by the CEO because they are friends. These friendships reinforce the entrenchment of management. One would hope, instead, that new directors would be chosen based on shareholder nomination or following a search by a professional search firm.

Research has found, perhaps surprisingly, that outside

directors on the board—as opposed to insiders—have a negative effect on company performance. This finding is hard to unpack with confidence, but the authors of the study that uncovered this relationship speculate that perhaps boards are expanded for political reasons, not because the outside directors will be helpful in guiding the firm, and are thus detrimental when it comes to performance.[47]

Share ownership is another important thing to look for in a board. Some boards have members with minimal share ownership. This can mean that incentives are not well-aligned. Sometimes there is a family running the board, with a substantial ownership interest. This can be a positive but is not always. What is more important is whether the family is engaged and interested in growing long-term shareholder value. Family members may have their own idiosyncratic interests that do not line up with investor needs.

Activists and venture capitalists can be board members and often own substantial numbers of shares. They can be very valuable board members, as they are usually highly motivated to grow shareholder value. On boards, or working outside of the board structure, many activists end up not being very effective. Activists believe that they can increase shareholder value by changing management—either practices or personnel—and make a profit for themselves and other shareholders, but their plans are not always beneficial. The best activists and activist firms look for conflicts of interest between management and shareholders and proceed to involve themselves in these situations. These do tend to be most effective when the activists own significant share percentages. It is difficult to organize large numbers of small shareholders to take decisive action against management that is destroying shareholder value. It is much easier when there are a few large shareholders in place.

In my experience, the most successful activist campaigns involve an attempt to get the company to do one of two things: either divest a significant business or put the whole company up for sale. There have been situations where an activist-driven management change proved to be very successful for shareholders, though there are certainly many other situations where it did not. Activists on the board can put pressure on management to improve its performance.

Activist hedge funds, as David Larcker has discussed in his book, *Corporate Governance Matters*, "resemble value investors, targeting companies that have relatively high profitability ... [but] have underperformed in the market." These hedge funds meet their objectives 60 percent of the time, but, at least in one study, the net value creation of hedge fund activism was found to be zero. Activists in the aggregate neither benefit nor harm shareholders, though their campaigns do tend to be quite costly.[48]

Then again, the individual results can absolutely vary. Canadian Pacific is an example where even a well-run company—ranked fourth out of 250 Canadian companies in the *Globe and Mail* corporate governance rankings in 2011—can be targeted by activists in a way that yields a positive outcome for shareholders.[49] Activist investor Bill Ackman believed the company was underperforming compared with competitor railways and wrote a letter to shareholders disparaging the performance of the

CEO and the board. The CEO ended up resigning, and five board members did not stand for reelection. Ackman's nominees were voted in instead. Five years later, in 2016, Ackman sold his shares, having generated a compounded annualized shareholder return of 45.39 percent, far exceeding the relevant index, and Ackman's fund earned $2.6 billion.[50] As it happens, six years later, in 2022, Ackman decided to return to Canadian Pacific and became one of its largest shareholders once again.[51]

How a board is compensated can affect the strength of its performance. Sometimes the entire board is compensated with shares, and the directors hold them for the long term. Generally, the more concentrated the share ownership, the stronger the governance. Very large companies with fragmented share ownership can lead to situations where management is entrenched and not particularly responsive: they don't need to be when there are no apparent consequences at stake. Research indeed shows that stock-based compensation for outside directors is effective in aligning their interests with stockholders and boosting firm performance.[52]

Especially in foreign countries, it is worth examining whether the "independent" directors are truly independent. In my experience, there are many independent directors who have ties back to the company, often through companies that perform the corporate audits, investment banking services, banking or legal services, or some other financial link. In some cases, these are disclosed in company documents, but in many foreign countries, there is no such disclosure. Research shows that there is potential for cronyism when it comes to board compensation: director compensation and CEO compensation were found to be linked, and excessive compensation was correlated with negative firm performance.[53]

It is also worth considering why the directors want their positions. For some directors, there is a professional desire to be informed about another company or its technology in order to be better executives at their own company. Some are directors for reasons of prestige. Some perform the task because they themselves are shareholders and truly care about the corporate outcomes. Some directors are directors solely for the compensation. Other individuals exist as professional directors. Some caution should be exercised around many of these categories—directors who want to gain more directorships, or have something to gain by remaining a director, may be reluctant to rock the boat, even if the situation calls for intervention. Research shows that the performance of the companies on whose boards a director sits does in fact correlate with the director's future appointment to more boards, meaning that incentives are aligned for directors who aspire to gain more directorships.[54]

On the other hand, it has been shown in the research that busy boards—boards filled with directors whose energies are mostly spent elsewhere—hurt corporate performance. In "Are Busy Boards Effective Monitors?" the authors write, "Firms with busy boards, those in which a majority of outside directors hold three or more directorships, are associated with weak corporate governance . . . lower market-to-book ratios, weaker profitability, and lower sensitivity of CEO turnover to firm performance."[55]

International Considerations

Corporate governance is reasonably standard in the United States, constrained in some respects due to the presence of activist investors, with the range of accounting treatments constrained by various regulatory requirements. There simply isn't a great deal of variation. This is not necessarily true abroad. Outside of the US, there is a wide range of variation in both governance and accounting, which provides greater potential to add real value through fundamental research.

While in Anglo-Saxon countries (UK/US/Canada/Australia/New Zealand) there is a clear expectation that the shareholders "own" the company, in the rest of the world there exists a variety of structures. In Germany, for instance, there is a two-tiered board system that requires labor representation. In Japan, there is the expectation that labor is a corporate stakeholder. In many countries, there are poorly developed or corrupt judiciaries, which further complicate the question of who actually "owns" the company.

What this ultimately means is that the proportion of companies where there is no controlling shareholder is much higher in the Anglo-Saxon countries, as well as Switzerland and France. Elsewhere, there are much larger percentages of companies that are controlled by wealthy families, financial institutions, or the government. The following chart illustrates the proportions of a range of ownership models around the world.[56]

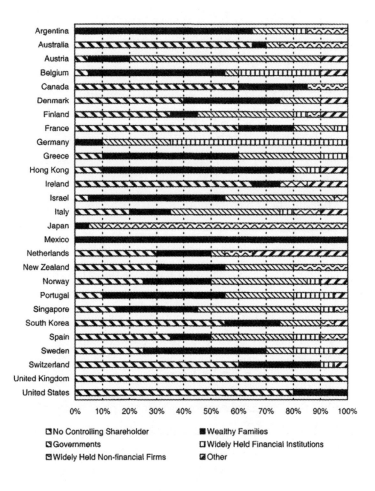

Who controls the world's great corporations?

Sources: La Porta et al. (1999) with Japanese data augmented by Morck and Nakamura (1999) to account for combined *keiretsu* stakes and German data augmented with information from Baums (1995) to account for bank proxy voting.

Notes: Fraction of top ten firms with different types of controlling shareholders is shown for each country. Control is assumed if any shareholder or group of shareholders believed to work in consort controls 20 percent of the votes in a company's annual shareholder meeting.

The Anglo-Saxon countries also tend to have judiciaries that are relatively impartial and follow the law. This is also true of Switzerland, and relatively true of France. The Anglo-Saxon countries plus Western Europe and Japan, with some exceptions for Spain, Portugal, and Italy, adhere to the rule of law and are less corrupt compared to the rest of the world.

This makes investing in companies from these countries often more desirable. There is a strong argument to make for the efficiency of public companies without a controlling shareholder. The capital asset pricing model—"an idealized portrayal of how financial markets price securities and thereby determine expected returns on capital investments," according to *Harvard Business Review*[57]—tells us that only nondiversifiable risk is priced, while other risk can be diversified away.

In other words, there is a deadweight loss when the rule of law is not clear and enforced or where poor legal systems or poor corporate governance restrict the efficiency of public companies that have dispersed ownership. Companies operating in these countries sometimes end up resorting to alternative forms of corporate control in order to remain efficient:

- Family control of companies
- Control by financial institutions
- Government control
- Large groups of companies with interlocking ownership

Each of these alternative models has flaws. David Larcker has written about family ownership making controlling members risk averse on the one hand, but he finds that family firms perform better than nonfamily firms *when the family member serves as CEO*.[58] Indeed, studies have found that there is concern when companies pass to the next generation. The presence of a founding family is value-enhancing when the *founder* is the firm's chairman or CEO, but there is a negative impact when a *descendant* of the founder is leading the firm instead.[59]

The financial institution model is flawed because it usually involves money-lending by the financial institution and can result in a company being run far more conservatively than would be optimal in order to minimize the potential that any loans will not be able to be repaid. Government control can lead companies to pursue objectives that are not shareholder friendly and driven by political agendas or the need to create or preserve jobs at all costs. Often, the government will have special rights to nominate or appoint directors, and such directors are rarely advocates for long-term shareholder value. Instead, they seek policies that are politically popular or otherwise serve the interest of the government—and, in some cases, can facilitate corruption. State-owned banks are especially dangerous because lending can be driven by political considerations, leading to an accumulation of bad debts. Poor regulation can lead to these bad debts not being recognized to the point where a company can wind up with a negative value.

Of course, government-regulated industries don't just exist outside of the Anglo-Saxon world. Regulated industries anywhere in the world lead to similar concerns. They tend to not only be politically influenced, with political appointees often on the board, but the regulation also reduces competition and potentially slows innovation by restricting entry of new competitors. Deregulation is the enemy of established companies in a regulated industry. We can look at what happened to the savings and loan industry when it was deregulated—the savings and loan crisis of the 1980s, where hundreds of banks failed[60]—or at the natural gas industry or electric utilities for more examples of how deregulation led to a wider range of outcomes for industry participants. Bond investors, for instance, are often helped by regulation since it provides stability. There is a rich literature on how regulators are often captured by the industry at issue, leading to higher profits.

Some boards throughout the world also include labor representatives. While these representatives often have an interest in seeing the company succeed, they are generally more focused on improving working conditions as opposed to shareholder value. Large groups of companies with interlocking ownership is a system often seen in Japan. This can lead to suboptimal insulation from the kind of shareholder pressure that might increase shareholder value.

Japan is a particularly interesting example in a number of ways. There has been an evolution in Japan from exceptionally poor governance to governance that is slowly improving—leading to some real opportunities for investors. I was in a meeting once with a Japanese management team. The company had accumulated a very large amount of cash for no apparent reason, and we showed them how much shareholder value could be created by repurchasing shares. The CEO told me, "This is not your cash; this is our cash." No US management team would ever say something like this, and I think it is becoming rarer in Japan as well.

It is notable to look at the market value of publicly traded companies versus GDP in various countries. The Anglo-Saxon countries and Switzerland have higher percentages of market capitalization to GDP than the other countries, again due to shareholder primacy combined with a relative lack of corruption and a stable rule of law. As an investor, when one looks outside of these countries, it is worth spending more time on researching corporate governance. As one looks to invest in the emerging markets, one needs to be aware that corruption may be flourishing, and the likelihood of having a commercial dispute resolved fairly is diminished—so corporate governance becomes extremely important.

The value of good corporate governance varies by country. In North American and European countries, governance is generally rated as comparatively less important than other financial factors. As one moves to countries that have a less well-developed rule of law, governance becomes much more important. Reliance on the legal system in many of these countries is fraught with peril. Hence, governance at the corporate level is far more important.

With all of this taken together, there is significant evidence that good corporate governance leads to higher valuations, especially in countries where legal and market institutions are weaker. The McKinsey Investor Survey on Corporate Governance yields findings that governance is even more important than financials, particularly in emerging markets, and that investors will often pay significant premiums for well-governed businesses.[61]

In addition, research has found that even in countries where good corporate governance is not required by law, the existence of growth opportunities, the need for external financing, and concentrated ownership all lead to better governance practices.[62] These effects are even stronger in countries with weak standards, showing that companies will rise above the legal requirements when there are good reasons to do so.

The World Management Survey notes that US companies tend to be much more efficient than most foreign corporations. This may be due largely to better governance in the US.[63]

For further reading on international governance considerations, David Larcker and Bryan Tayan's book *Corporate Governance Matters* is an excellent choice. *A History of Corporate Governance around the World*, edited by Randall Morck, provides a good backdrop for how different forms of corporate governance evolved. *International Corporate Governance*, by Thomas Clarke, and *Handbook on International Corporate Governance*, edited by Christine Mallin, both provide a comparative view on systems of corporate governance around the world.[64]

Self-Dealing

Finally, an issue we find too often in emerging markets—but certainly not exclusively there—is self-dealing. The typical case is when there is a public company controlled by an individual or family and that same individual or family has private holdings in which their ownership stake may be higher. Transactions are then made between the public company and the private companies on terms that are quite unfavorable to the public shareholders. This unfairly enriches the controlling individual or family. Obviously, any situation where this kind of behavior may be at play is one to avoid as an investor.

Sometimes this plays out in somewhat less obvious ways. There are a fair number of companies, both in developed and developing markets, that have multiple share classes. There are some stock exchanges that refuse to list companies with multiple share classes, viewing it as bad corporate governance, which it often is. Companies with multiple share classes, where some classes have supervoting power, are a problem for governance. What they do is entrench management. Often, founders retain the supervoting power for their shares, making it impossible for outside activists or others to acquire the company and take control, even when it would serve shareholders for them to do so. In some overseas markets, there is also the situation in which a public holding company has the majority of its shares owned by an individual or family, and then there is a subsidiary company whose shares are majority-owned by the holding company. These situations both allow a minority of economic shares to control a majority of voting shares.

This can be useful in allowing a founder or a family to pursue its own vision of long-term success of the business without the potential distraction that activist investors might create. But the downside is that it prevents any market discipline from being enforced on the group that controls the assets. Investors need to be sure that the control group is aligned with the long-term shareholders. Any lack of alignment will not be able to be rectified by trying to change the board or management team.

A current example of investors wrestling with issues created by multiple share classes is in the case of Facebook/Meta. Its share classes allow Mark Zuckerberg to have virtually complete control of the company. If investors agree with his vision, this is fine, but in recent years, he has decided to pursue a strategy targeting the Metaverse, diverting resources from the existing (and profitable) social media businesses of Facebook and Instagram. In a public company with a single share class, it is unlikely that Mr. Zuckerberg would find it possible to redirect these resources toward pursuing the Metaverse; activist investors would almost certainly pursue campaigns to stop this investment. But the dual share class prevents any such action. Potential investors must decide whether they are comfortable with Mr. Zuckerberg being in absolute control before they make their investment.

Another example, a rather tragic one from a few decades ago, is Wang Labs. An Wang was a brilliant inventor and businessman, the genius behind "core memory," the first electronic calculator that could do logarithms, and the word processor. He built Wang Labs into a major corporation—and had a dual share class to protect the company from external pressures. At its peak, Wang Labs employed over thirty-three thousand people. But as An Wang aged, he made one fateful choice and handed control of the company to his son, Fred. Charles C. Kenney's 1992 book about the company remarks that "by almost any definition, [Fred was] unsuited for the job in which his father had placed him."[65] Fred's forced ascent led to the resignations of top executives and a downward spiral from which the company could not recover—not even after An Wang eventually fired Fred in 1989, a year before

An Wang died. Wang Labs filed for bankruptcy three years later, in 1992.

One final example that fits this pattern is News Corp. In 2011, News Corp, controlled by Rupert Murdoch, decided to purchase Murdoch's daughter Elisabeth's media company, Shine. Previously, Murdoch had purchased his son James's record company, Rawkus, which was eventually closed. Rupert Murdoch has employed all three of his children as executives and board members.

This is clearly governance that leaves something to be desired.

All the proper elements can be in place, yet if a company is improperly valued, it will not be a good investment. We look at valuation in the next chapter.

CHAPTER 5
VALUATION

When looking at valuation, people often start with the basic metrics, such as price to earnings, price to cash flow, price to book value, or price to sales. The success of these simple valuation metrics is highlighted in the book *What Works on Wall Street*, by James P. O'Shaughnessy.[1] Indeed, looking at the historical data, as recently as 2008, one would have confidently said that these ratios had performed well over time. But since 2008, it has been a bit of a different story. With the advent of quantitative firms, these simple valuation metrics may no longer work. The quantitative firms compete away the profits from these simple metrics. Book-to-market ratios, for instance, have now been shown to be worse over time at forecasting future returns and growth.[2] You can no longer outperform the market just by focusing on simple ratios. Quantitative funds jump on every possible anomaly and make it very hard to win on data alone.

At the same time, there are also some very real, substantive drawbacks to most of the standard valuation metrics. One is that they fail to look at what a company might have sacrificed from a forward-looking perspective in order to achieve current results. We can, for instance, look at an oil company that may have very strong earnings and cash flow right now as compared with its peers, but to achieve those numbers, has it sacrificed investment in exploration and the development of fields for the future? We need to pay attention not just to what a company is doing now but to whether its cash flow is sustainable over time—and that means looking at whether it has invested money and effort in the right places to maintain and grow the business. Merely looking at ratios does not address that issue.

Beyond this, another factor to consider is that physical assets have become a smaller and smaller portion of the capital stock of large American corporations, and intangible assets, like R&D and the power of a brand name, have become more valuable pieces of the portfolio. This is not captured in ratios like price to book. Book value is largely about physical assets, and accountants have real problems putting valuations on intangibles. There is no accepted way to do this. A company may have spent a tremendous amount on R&D, but you can't be sure it will turn into anything useful.

Patents

Patents are particularly hard things to value. They are sometimes the most valuable assets a company owns and sometimes have no added value at all. There are a number of approaches that have been suggested for valuing patents, but the lack of certainty about their value vexes accountants and leads to problems. Accountants dislike uncertainty, so they can sometimes disregard the very real value of some patents, even as they have become an increasingly large proportion of the value of some companies. There is evidence that properly incorporating the value of patents can make a significant difference in terms of stock bidding.

Some have offered the idea that patents can be valued by looking at other patents that cite them. This is an admittedly crude method of evaluating patent value, but given the scope of patents at some firms, it can be useful. Ultimately, what you want to understand is the future stream of cash flows from the patent. This can be very hard to determine as an outsider, so even a rough metric can be of some use.

It should be noted that it is not the number of patents that matters but the nature and motivation behind them. IBM, at one point, was paying bonuses based on the number of patents employees generated, which, of course, led to an increase in the number of patents filed. This might have helped generate additional licensing dollars in the short run, but it did little to sustain IBM's technological relevance. Indeed, Darío Gil, IBM's SVP and the director of IBM Research, admitted as much in an article in *Fortune* in early 2023: "As part of our relentless capacity for reinvention, we decided in 2020 that we would no longer pursue the goal of numeric patent leadership . . . . Patents are only one measure of a company's true capacity for innovation. IBM will continue to patent new technology, but patents alone are a more incomplete barometer than ever before."[3]

AOL is an example of a company that monetized its patent portfolio. It developed a number of valuable patents at the early stages of the internet and then sold them at a substantial valuation later on, unloading most of them to Microsoft for over $1 billion when AOL was struggling financially.[4]

Other Hard-to-Value Attributes

Every industry potentially has elements that are important for valuation but not captured in traditional metrics. For instance, when looking at cellular operators, the value of the spectrum is quite important, or for companies selling forest products, the valuation per acre of woods can be quite critical. Natural resources under a company's control are hard to value but are often very important. There can be a benefit to looking at valuation from a number of different perspectives and not just relying on one or a handful of metrics. Some metrics will be favorable, and others may expose real weaknesses; the trick is to take them each as individual inputs and consider how they fit into the larger picture.

Implied Valuation

Looking at the implied value of a company can also be a useful piece of information. You can do this by taking some simple valuation metrics and running an appropriate regression to yield the information you're looking for. At one point in my career, I ran an analysis to look at the implied price of debt, imagining that $1 of debt would be valued at $1 in the marketplace. It turned out that debt fluctuated in value over time quite significantly. Right before the 2008 financial crisis, debt was discounted by a very small percentage of what it was actually worth, and then after the crisis, debt became much more negatively valued because no one wanted indebted companies anymore. Looking at some of these metrics over time can provide insight into what is and isn't being valued by investors.

You can do the same thing with accruals, or commercial real estate, for instance. Commercial real estate valuations fluctuated quite a bit around the time of the commercial real estate crisis in the early 1990s.

Valuation is hard to do well, but it is a critical component in any analysis. It is also the case that sometimes you may be able to effectively determine a company's current value but are unsure of how that will change in the future. In the next chapter, we look at forecasting future value and the biases that can affect us all.

CHAPTER 6
FORECASTING

Forecasting accurately is extremely challenging. I once undertook a project where I looked at analyst forecasts over time and discovered—as others have as well—that the ability of analysts to forecast earnings even just one year out is not very good, and the ability to forecast more than one year out is basically nonexistent. If someone tells you they can forecast accurately, you should be extremely skeptical.

The master researcher and writer in the domain of forecasting is Philip Tetlock, author of a number of impressive books, including *Superforecasting: The Art and Science of Prediction*.[1] I met Tetlock when he spoke to our research group at an off-site event. Good forecasting, Tetlock has found, involves the incorporation of evidence from a range of sources, relying on probabilistic thinking, working in teams rather than alone, keeping track of results, and, what I think is most important, being able to admit when you are wrong and revise your predictions.

There are people who have very strong opinions about all kinds of things, and if you are unable to change your mind as new information becomes available, that is a very dangerous trait. Having worked with many people over the years who have expressed opinions about companies and industries, I have found that people who have very strong opinions often look for information that supports those opinions and disregard information that doesn't support their views. Their opinions thus stay the same, regardless of the existence of contrary information. Silicon Valley forecaster Paul Saffo, who teaches at Stanford, writes about strong opinions weakly held. "Allow your intuition to guide you to a conclusion," he offers, "no matter how imperfect—this is the 'strong opinion' part. Then—and this is the 'weakly held' part—prove yourself wrong. Engage in creative doubt. Look for information that doesn't fit, or indicators that [point] in an entirely different direction."[2]

Philip Tetlock finds that people who remain objective and continue to incorporate new information regardless of whether it supports their hypothesis are much better forecasters than people with strongly held opinions. He also finds that people who forecast based on granular, objective information are better forecasters than people who go with their gut or who don't forecast on granularity. If there is data available that can inform your opinions, use the data and build forecasts up from that data, even if it goes against your instincts.

Behavioral Biases: Recency Bias

Nobel Prize laureate economist Robert Shiller has taught at Yale since 1982. He presented a paper more than twenty-five years ago titled, "Human Behavior and the Efficiency of the Financial System," and his takeaways have stuck with me ever since.[3] One is that many analysts get overly caught up in recent numbers and give them too much credence when thinking about the long term. Back in the year 2000, a friend of mine looked at the previous twenty-five years of S&P performance and found that the most successful company had been Walmart. Walmart had grown quickly and been quite profitable. My friend then looked at the forecasts for other S&P companies and found that a full one-third of the S&P was priced as if the companies were forecasted to grow in the future even faster than Walmart had grown in the past. This would have been an impossible outcome, for a third of all companies to grow faster than the most successful company over the previous quarter-century had grown. But not many of us stop and think about the full range of possibilities when making forecasts and how likely an extreme result really is.

Making sure to maintain a historical perspective, and having an incredibly strong case for why a particular company might be likely to be an extreme outlier, if you are, in fact, forecasting it to be one, is very important.

Behavioral Biases: Prospect Theory

Shiller also discusses prospect theory, developed by Daniel Kahneman and Amos Tversky in 1979. Prospect theory in part describes the phenomenon that we tend to underweight "extremely improbable" outcomes, deciding they will never happen, and overweight "extremely probable" outcomes, assuming they are certain to occur.[4] I like to think about a semiconductor company I know of that turned into a hamburger chain—in effect, the semiconductor company had accumulated huge tax losses and was acquired by the burger chain for its tax loss carry-forward. It was an unusual situation, to say the least, but unusual doesn't mean impossible. When we ignore the black swans, we take a huge risk because the improbable cases may well be disasters, and if you have a highly levered company in a cyclical business, it could go bankrupt and you could be left with nothing.

Behavioral Biases: Regret Theory

Regret theory plays a role in Shiller's work as well. We don't like to be wrong, so we tend to avoid admitting errors, or, as Shiller mentions, selling stocks at a loss to lock in the certainty that buying them was a mistake.[5] We also learn, over time, to avoid the pain of regret by making conservative predictions that are unlikely to be terribly incorrect. I read an interesting paper years ago along these lines, about how experienced professionals tend to make conservative forecasts, and the boldest, most extreme forecasts are made by less experienced people, at least in part to attract attention and position themselves as heroes if the low-probability outcome does, in fact, come true. They forecast an unlikely case and, like a lottery, hope for the best.

Behavioral Biases: Failure to Incorporate New Information

There is plenty of literature on how we assume that the current state of affairs will continue forever, which contributed to the mortgage crisis, where people assumed the default rate on residential mortgages would be low forever. There is evidence that over the short term, security prices tend to underreact to new information for exactly this reason. If there is information that contradicts people's current beliefs, we tend to be slow to believe the new information, assuming that what we know already is both correct and likely to continue to be correct. Eventually, if reality is, in fact, in conflict with our perception, the market does catch up—but it often takes longer than it should.

Behavioral Biases: Disjunction Effect

Shiller writes as well about the disjunction effect, which is something I've witnessed many times in my career, at huge detriment to the people succumbing to this important behavioral bias. The disjunction effect is the urge to want to wait to make a decision until you collect new information, even if you've already made a justifiable choice.[6] I've seen analysts make a compelling case to invest in a company but insist that they want to wait until the company has a management meeting in a few weeks, just to be sure. In the normal course of decision-making, this might be unproblematic, but when it comes to the financial markets, it is devastating. The entire point of research and information-gathering is to be ahead of the market and see more than other investors. If you wait until the meeting, everyone else will see the value of the investment, too, and the advantage you would get from jumping in early will be lost. Reality will already be incorporated into the price. The time to act instead is now, even if you'd feel better emotionally with more information or have an urge to validate your findings.

Behavioral Biases:
Social Contagion and Validation

Schiller writes about social contagion,[7] which has played a significant role in the work I've done over the years. If you look at some of the big hedge funds, there are absolutely cases where someone gets excited about a particular company and tries to promote it with other firms. I have had many instances where people came to me and tried to make the case that we should join them in an investment position where they had already made their buy. We see social contagion play out in the extreme in cases like GameStop, AMC, or other meme stocks. Individuals influence each other on social media sites, and investors rush in at the same time, driving prices way up based not on fundamentals but on chatter and internet attention. This occurs even among professionals, who, wanting to belong to a crowd, generate support for their position or validate a decision they've made.

This desire for validation is common. People want others they respect to agree with them, either to justify their thinking or to give them cover in case they're wrong. "How could you blame me for this when Warren Buffett felt exactly the same way?" they imagine as a perfect defense.

Of course, the best way to make money in the financial markets isn't to have an opinion that others agree with; it's to have an opinion completely at odds with everyone else, and at the same time to have that opinion turn out right. That's how you make money. But it's hard for a lot of people to do that because they start to doubt themselves. As George Soros has said, "Money is made by discounting the obvious and betting on the unexpected."[8] Look for reasons why others might be wrong, and start your analysis there instead of hoping for validation.

Sources of Information

As mentioned, one of Philip Tetlock's principles is to incorporate information from a range of sources. This can include SEC financials, investor call transcripts, company and competitor presentations, conversations with investor relations departments, and more. There is also a point to make about the wisdom of crowds. You do not have to make investing decisions in a vacuum and, in fact, should not. There is value in debate and in testing your thinking with others.

One freely accessible source I have found surprisingly helpful—and often quite powerful for the long-term investor—is Glassdoor, which provides employees with the opportunity to post reviews online.[9] This gives the investor an opportunity to get a true employee perspective on what it is like to work at the company. For most large companies, there are a significant number of comments posted on Glassdoor. Even some relatively small companies have a meaningful number of Glassdoor reviews.

These reviews can provide insights into employee morale as well as opinions of management and the company's business prospects.

In the fall of 2013, the *Los Angeles Times* published stories on fraudulent accounts being set up at Wells Fargo bank.[10] These accounts were the result of immense pressure put on employees to increase the number of products purchased per customer. The news seemed to come out of nowhere and launched a huge scandal for the bank. However, if one looks at the Glassdoor reviews prior to the initial article, there was already mention of the problem. After the *LA Times* pieces, Wells Fargo stock grossly underperformed, and numerous regulatory problems affected the company and management for years. Yet the information investors could have discovered in advance was hiding in plain sight.

The unfortunate truth is that when there are issues with a company's integrity, the first sign of trouble is rarely the only one. A long-term investor should avoid companies that have a fundamental integrity issue, at least until management has been completely replaced. Cultural issues are not easily fixed. But the information is often out there if you look for it. Another example along the same lines as Wells Fargo is DXC Technology (DXC). Mike Lawrie was the CEO of DXC, which was formed after the merger of Computer Sciences Corp and the Enterprise Services Division of Hewlett-Packard. Lawrie embarked on a fairly draconian cost-cutting program and promoted it relentlessly in the analyst community. At the same time, Glassdoor reviews of the company showed a drastically lower opinion of DXC as a place to work compared to what one might expect in the industry.

Comments also pointed to a low level of respect for management. This was a sign that the story that Lawrie and DXC were telling analysts was an unsustainable one and may not have actually been the truth.

As it turned out, Lawrie was pursuing an unsustainable set of employee practices. The company's valuation rose—from 20 to 30 percent of sales to over 100 percent of sales—from the bright future that Lawrie painted, but then reality set in. Lawrie was accused in the press of "having a 'toxic' management style" and "verbally abusing" those under him.[11] The company was sued by one manager who claimed he was fired for pushing back against the speed at which Lawrie wanted to lay off workers and argued that the vesting dates for his share grants were changed in order to avoid paying him $20 million in severance.[12] This was just the tip of the iceberg. The share price soon collapsed.

The academic evidence backs up the idea that crowdsourced employer reviews make a difference when forecasting performance going forward. A 2018 paper found that "firms experiencing improvements in crowdsourced employer ratings significantly outperform firms with declines . . . . Employer rating changes are associated with growth in sales and profitability and help forecast one-quarter-ahead earnings announcement surprises."[13]

It is likely that more sources of online information will show themselves valuable over time, and we should remain alert as to how to utilize new information as it presents itself. Specifically with regard to Glassdoor, how employees feel is absolutely a factor that is relevant to company success. Drastic restructuring is occasionally necessary, and will never be popular, but there are risks. It is important to consider whether the restructuring has an endpoint. Making employees feel overworked and miserable, to an extent that they won't recommend their employer to a friend, is not sustainable for a business. Companies that have low ratings on Glassdoor should be approached with extreme caution.

Base Rates

The concept of base rates refers to looking at the data of similar companies to establish a baseline expectation for performance. Michael Mauboussin, head of consilient research at Counterpoint Global, Morgan Stanley Investment Management, and the author of numerous valuable books on investing, originally brought this concept to popular attention.[14] For this discussion, the point to understand is that it is unrealistic to expect a company to have a dramatically better outcome than other similar companies. One example, which I will discuss in more detail in the chapter to come on risk, is Silicon Valley Bank. How could it have grown so quickly when other banks hadn't? This alone should have been a clue that something was amiss.

We can look at a company in any industry and examine how its most successful competitors have grown. If you are forecasting your company to grow at a much faster rate than any company in your industry has ever grown, there has to be a terrific reason why. The same goes for levels of profitability or pretty much any other outcome. Why will your company be so different, even in success? It's very hard for one company to suddenly and dramatically outperform any similar company's past results, so if you are basing decisions on expectations like that, you have to ask yourself how likely this really is to happen.

I remember Motorola during the peak of the internet bubble. Its shares sold for $60 each, and if you predicted growth for the company at the fastest rate it had ever achieved in a three-year period, with the most profitability as it had ever achieved in a three-year period, and projected those numbers out for thirty years, you would still end up with a return lower than the thirty-year bond. This was a situation that was practically impossible to ever work out, but people still believed at the time that it could happen.

There is one particular question worth thinking about when looking at base rates: How asset-intensive is the company? If you have an oil or mining company, that is a very asset-intensive business. You have to buy the property, secure the leases, drill, etc. Each of these things costs a lot of money—which constrains how fast a company can grow. This is because the company needs to be generating cash in order to make these investments. On the other hand, with something like a software company or a drop-ship clothing company, where the company just does the designs and outsources the manufacturing, growth rates can be much higher. These companies can grow at an extremely rapid rate because there is basically no cost once you have the piece of software or the clothing design. This is very different for a company that needs to make physical investments. Drug companies are like software companies in this respect. Once you develop a drug (which can, of course, be very expensive, even as high as $1 billion to get it fully approved), manufacturing is very cheap, and the rate of growth can be extremely high with huge profits. You just need, as with the clothing or software company, to make that initial investment.

Along similar lines, the regulated return and dividend payouts of utilities companies can severely limit their growth potential, but nevertheless multiples on utilities earnings are often exceptionally high. In contrast, bank multiples can be exceptionally low even as their capacity to expand loan growth or return capital to shareholders is meaningfully higher.

As we move toward an economy driven more and more by IP and brand names, there is potential for wider variation in growth rates. Brand names and IP are more like software and drug companies—no cost once developed and the sky is the limit, as opposed to companies that are asset-intensive. Moët Hennessy Louis Vuitton (LVMH) is a case study in the value of brands. The company, with almost two hundred thousand employees worldwide, runs a portfolio of seventy-five of the most prestigious and luxurious brands in the world, including Tiffany & Co., Christian Dior, Sephora, Princess Yachts, TAG Heuer, and more. As the IBS Center for Management Research has written, "Brand building in the luxury business was challenging. Effectively, customer desire had to be created for things that were not really needed. [But] LVMH's business model attempted to define sharply the brand identity . . . [and] create brand excitement among customers."[15] This has become the way the company has generated tremendous value.

The final point here is that for all this discussion of how we can't ignore base rates, sometimes it is actually the case that companies do break from the past and have incredible results; this is where a bold prediction can be justified. I'm thinking about Microsoft and Intel, both of which had sharp breaks from past history—but the point is that there were reasons these outcomes happened, and it's rare. The fact that it's not a "never" outcome means people assume it will happen with their company—but it's rare enough that we have to be very careful when making predictions that outstrip all past performance.

Forecasting on the whole is risky simply because the future is inherently uncertain. You need to think probabilistically and make sure that even long-tail events are taken into consideration because they can ultimately be a company's downfall.

There are two more topics to cover in the book: sell discipline and risk. Both are critical to understanding when building an investment portfolio. You have to know when to sell, and you also need to realize that return is never guaranteed. Every investment, no matter how careful your research, will still carry significant risk.

CHAPTER 7
SELL DISCIPLINE

A 2021 study by the National Bureau of Economic Research revealed that fund managers over the past two decades had shown demonstrable skill in picking which stocks to buy—but performed terribly when it came to decisions to sell.[1] "Selling decisions not only fail to beat a no-skill random selling strategy," wrote the researchers, "they consistently underperform it."

I look back at my own experience, and it's easy to see why this is true. We make decisions to buy based on considerable research, with the universe of possibilities out there to choose from. We see the core of our job as finding the next big thing to add to the portfolio. But once we buy, the choice to sell is much more nuanced. In a perfect world, we buy a security, it goes up tremendously, and then, when we believe it has become severely overvalued, we sell.

But the point at which an investment has become overvalued is not always clear, and sometimes the fundamentals of the business change and start to deteriorate. When do you pull the plug? It can be embarrassing to sell if you haven't seen a gain—to lock in a loss plays into the behavioral biases discussed in the chapter on forecasting. But misjudgments happen all the time to professional investors. The best way to salvage a bad investment is to sell early, of course—ideally before the company has reported bad news and the change to the fundamentals that you have seen has been incorporated into the stock price. This is almost impossible to do. Even the most rational investor has a hard time reevaluating a stock he owns in a fully objective way. It is made even more difficult for professional investors because once they own stock in a company, they may begin to get to know the company's management and might even become friends with them. Management virtually always has good rationalizations for why bad news is only a temporary setback and why indications of underlying issues should not be trusted.

One needs a lot of self-discipline to move beyond these reasons to stay the course. When one spots a situation where fundamentals have seriously deteriorated, accounting is becoming questionable, management is destroying shareholder value through acquisitions or other questionable practices, or technology has changed to the disadvantage of the company—just to name a few potential flags—the correct answer is always to sell. But deciding whether a declining stock means a problem worth taking action over or an opportunity to buy more at a reduced price is always a tricky decision that requires serious investigation and thought. It is important to take emotion out of it. If you would not buy were you not already invested, it is often a signal to think about selling. The reality is that less time is spent on sell theses than buy theses. When this is because valuation has gone up, usually this is fine, but you run the risk of missing a company in transition and selling too soon or missing a situation where underlying business factors have changed but are not yet reflected in the stock price, meaning you may end up selling too late.

CHAPTER 8
RISK

As a final chapter in this book, we need to consider investment risk. Investment risk is often misunderstood. Many investors, even sophisticated ones, will focus on certain types of risks but ignore others that are just as important, if not more so. Some investors will look back at past results and discount the possibility that the future will unfold quite differently. Others might be swayed by their own wishful thinking or personal biases about what risks are legitimate to consider and what seems unlikely to happen. The entire point of thinking about risk is that we don't know what the future will be and need to pay attention not just to the information we already know but to the information that is unknowable.

In this last chapter, I will discuss a number of types of risk that should be at the forefront of any investment evaluation. We cannot make successful investment decisions without a healthy understanding of risks and rewards. Complete absence of risk is unavoidable. But by appreciating the scope of what we can't predict, we can make smarter (and often more diversified) choices for our portfolios.

Market Risk (Beta)

Beta (β) is a measure of the volatility—or risk—of a particular investment compared to the market as a whole. Higher beta means more volatility. But while beta can provide some information about risk, it is based on looking backward, and past statistical relationships may not hold in the future. Relationships measured over shorter time periods are particularly vulnerable to this issue.

The reality is that even if beta was a perfect measure, conditions change, whether in the broader economy, in particular industries, or for individual companies. A company may decide to leverage itself, changing the risk significantly. Industries can perform quite differently at different points in an economic cycle. Vulnerability to changes in interest rates may not manifest themselves until interest rates actually change. The economy is dynamic—with an impossibly large number of variables at play. Relying too heavily on measures like beta is a trap for those who blindly assume that past performance is always going to be a useful guide. For instance, pre- and post-2008, the betas of bank stocks increased quite dramatically.[1]

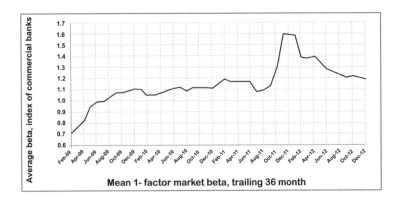

Pricing models are based on looking backward in time and don't allow for the dynamic repricing of investments. In the finance world, models are built around value at risk—a statistic that measures the extent of possible financial losses—and while it has some use, the formula doesn't allow for breakdowns in historical relationships between investments. And sometimes those relationships do break down. We can look at the example of Long-Term Capital Management (LTCM)—a highly leveraged hedge fund that was started by Salomon Brothers' head of bond trading, John Meriwether, along with Nobel laureates Myron Scholes and Robert C. Merton (famous for the Black-Scholes stock pricing model). The fund was built on the historical relationships between investments, and by 1997–1998, the relationships started to break down, returns got worse, and everyone began to pull money out at once, leading to the fund's collapse.

What happened in the past is simply not a risk-free predictor of what will happen in the future. You end up with 1-in-10,000 and 1-in-100,000 events happening at a rate they mathematically shouldn't. The odds don't make sense, given the limited number of observations. The models fail to recognize the interdependence of different factors and how crises can snowball. When LTCM began having success, other funds followed with a similar model—and when one blew up, the rest of them did as well, with clients asking for their money back everywhere at the same time. The market ends up making seemingly independent events not independent at all.

The reality is that measures of market risk do not always end up telling us truly useful things about the comparative risks of investments. For instance, the theory of mean reversion posits that extreme deviations in the changing of certain values—whether high or low—are likely to revert to their historical averages over time.[2] But only some types of investments are mean-reverting in theory—and when you compare the risk of an investment that ought to be expected to mean-revert (a value stock, for instance, bought at an undervalued price) to one that should not be mean-reverting (a growth stock, for instance, bought to capitalize on future possibilities not reflected in past results), you can run into trouble. There is a real problem in comparing the time-series results of value managers and growth managers if you don't take into consideration this difference. The statistical measures of risk comparing the two portfolios will be flawed—and extending the measurement window (to quarters or months instead of days) will change the outcome in some cases quite significantly. If a series is mean-reverting, then extending the measurement period will reduce risk relative to a series that is not mean-reverting.

Risk of Permanent Loss of Capital

We often underestimate—or at least do not fully appreciate—the risk of permanent loss of capital, and thus the value of holding investments that carry a much lower risk of going to zero. A necessary business that is not levered or leveraged—meaning it is not carrying debt—will ultimately have some underlying value. Investing in a highly levered business—with debt that might even exceed equity—may result in the permanent loss of capital.

For example: High-quality agricultural property, if unlevered, will always have some value. It may become overvalued (due, perhaps, to unreasonably low interest rates), but it should never fall to zero. On the other hand, an industry that is endangered by technological change, deregulation (including trade agreements), or other seismic economic shifts may become worthless. (Once again, statistical measures of beta may not capture this. An industry may be relatively low risk measured statistically until there is some underlying technological change or deregulation that radically changes the landscape.)

The issue here is not just volatility—levered and nonlevered securities can both be quite volatile—but rather the endpoint if things don't go well. A necessary business will have ultimate value. Even if one purchases it when it is overvalued, the potential for permanent capital loss is limited—and even more so if you purchase it at a reasonable valuation.

Capital is also at risk when investing in a business that makes a product that is a fad or one that could become technologically obsolete—think about investors in Eastman Kodak. Eastman Kodak dominated the market for chemical photography from the early part of the twentieth century until nearly the end of it. But by the 1980s, electronic photography was gaining popularity. Kodak made some effort to diversify into the pharmaceutical market and to enter the electronic photography market. Eventually, the professional photography market became dominated by the Japanese consumer electronic companies. In the consumer market, it became a feature of a cell phone, and thus the value of Eastman Kodak's core business became quite limited. Eastman Kodak eventually filed for bankruptcy in 2012.

Even if a particular technology is here to stay, early market trends do not always play out over time, and many early entrants to any new industry will end up disappearing. In the early 1980s, personal computers were first becoming widely adopted. There were well over one hundred personal computer companies—yet the only one that still exists today is Apple (and it may well still exist due to other products such as the iPhone). Even then, you could be sure that the world did not need one hundred personal computer companies—and, indeed, most of them went to zero. A similar kind of issue exists today with cryptocurrencies. There are over ten thousand cryptocurrencies today.[3] Ten years from now, I suspect there will be only a handful of survivors.

Liquidity Risk

Some liquidity risk always exists. It is even observable in the Treasury market—see, for instance, the yield differential between on-the-run and off-the-run Treasury securities. This risk can be exaggerated in times of financial downturn, as many people try to raise funds at the same time. Liquidity risk can be affected by crowding. The number of strategies that rely on a particular investment can greatly affect the liquidity of that investment. What you want to avoid is everyone wanting to liquidate a particular investment at the same time. Strategies that are highly reliant on certain securities are most at risk.

Liquidity risk can also be affected by how many people can estimate the value of a particular investment, as well as how many owners will be subject to the same demands on their capital at the same time. A good example of problems that result when few people can estimate the value of an investment is the collateralized debt obligations/collateralized loan obligations (CDO/CLO) experience with mortgage-backed securities in 2008. Very few people understood how to value these securities. When they suddenly lost value, those same people were at the center of demands for the return of capital. It took some time for others to recognize the underlying value in those securities.

Short-Term versus Long-Term Risk

There are risk differences to consider when looking at short-term and long-term investments. A problem with long-tailed investments is that they may seem like a good idea when a project is started, but by the time that project is finished, the same investment may seem like an exceptionally bad idea. Commercial real estate projects have a long history of boom and bust. High rents signal to the marketplace that more buildings need to be constructed. But the same signal is available to all. If too many people act on the signal and start building commercial buildings of the same type, in the same area, then by the time they are all completed, there will be a glut of space, and rents may be too low to sustain all the properties constructed.

This played out in the late 1980s and early 1990s in a concrete way. As women began to enter the labor force in huge numbers in the mid-1970s, there needed to be a huge amount of growth in terms of office space. Combined with big tax advantages involved in the construction of office buildings, there was a huge boom—and, for a time, the investments were all incredibly profitable. Everyone thought office buildings were a great investment. But then markets got severely overbuilt, as the influx of new workers peaked and then slowed. In addition, the 1986 Tax Reform Act restricted some of the more egregious tax angles for office buildings. But once you've built the buildings, it's too late—you're stuck. In the late 1980s and early 1990s, there was a huge contraction in the value of commercial office space, and a number of banks failed as a result. People assumed that because lending money for commercial office space had been low risk for years, it would always be a smart investment—until the whole endeavor blew up and the market crashed.

We are likely set to see a similar market crash coming soon. The commercial office market is in real trouble. Vacancy rates are so high because so many people are now working from home. People hold loans on those office buildings, and they will have to be recorded as losses eventually, even if they haven't manifested themselves yet. Leases will expire and people won't renew them, and if you can't fill the building, it's going to go under.

We find a similar type of risk when we look at banks. Banks offer a commodity product: money. Due to deposit insurance, all banks can raise significant funds, assuming that their regulators allow them to. Regulators tend to be overly focused on capital ratios and past credit losses. They tend not to be very forward-looking in terms of evaluating risk. (As an aside, it is interesting to note that prior to deposit insurance, there were fewer bank failures.)

For many years, I was a bank stock analyst. To me, the greatest risk to banks was rapid loan growth—and it played out as the same kind of long-tail problem I've described. Some banks may be physically located in more attractive geographies, where the overall economy is growing more rapidly. Or some banks may specialize in a particular type of lending that is experiencing particularly rapid growth. However, rapid loan growth must be perceived as a risk. Banks are relatively constrained in terms of the interest rates they can offer. There is a competitive market for funds. Where they can deviate from one another instead is in the evaluation of credit risk. Rapid loan growth, particularly when compared to comparably situated banks, is almost always a function of lax credit standards. And the risk is exacerbated when the projects are long-tailed.

It can appear, possibly for a number of years, that the credit decisions have been smart. But the longer the period of outsized loan growth continues, the greater the risk. More and more loans end up failing as time progresses. Credit markets, in general, can make this same type of mistake. Freely available capital can exacerbate credit errors—particularly when the availability of credit effectively makes an asset worth more since it can be leveraged. This whole situation can reinforce distortions. As a set of assets is "worth more" due to the fact that the assets can be leveraged, a distorted signal is sent to the market that more of those assets need to be created.

We can look at an example that emerged just as I was writing this book: Silicon Valley Bank (SVB) grew at an astonishingly fast rate, its deposits from the end of 2019 to the end of 2022 doubling in value. The CEO held a very minimal amount of stock, so he wasn't really incentivized to make the company work out longer term (this goes back to a point made earlier, in the governance chapter). SVB took a lot of risks with its loan portfolio but also built a huge securities portfolio that was made up of long-dated Treasury securities. As interest rates went up, the value of those fell. The bank had been acting under the assumption things would always stay the same, which, of course, things never do. Its strategy made the bank very dependent on getting in new deposits, so when people started to question whether SVB was going to make it, given the rise in interest rates, the decline in the value of bonds the bank was holding, and the quality of the loan portfolio, depositors fled—and, of course, the more people fled, the more the bank needed to sell bonds to recognize their losses to gain more capital. It became an unstoppable spiral as people rushed to pull out as much money as possible, leading to a rapid collapse.

The reality is that if you look at the history of financial institutions, any bank that has grown faster than the industry over a long period of time has wound up failing. The regulators should have understood this, but they, just like Silicon Valley Bank itself, likely assumed rates would always stay low.

It is not surprising that some of the greatest credit market failures are around these and other types of long-tailed assets. There have been a number of credit events linked to ships—which take a long time to build, thus creating plenty of long-tailed risk. Shipping rates get very high, and everyone builds a lot of ships— and then there are too many ships, and big losses result.

We can also look at the internet bubble and the credit events around fiber-optic cable. The assumption was that the demand for fiber would be high going forward, so there was a great influx of capital into the industry. Yet, like many long-tailed assets, the supply eventually exceeded the demand, which resulted in large credit losses. There were also large losses on some of the internet companies during that boom. Sky-high valuations of equities led lenders to believe that there was considerable security for lending. Unfortunately, many of these companies simply disappeared once the bubble popped.

There are quite a few industries that are subject to this same type of long-tailed risk. Offshore oil platforms can take five to eight years to construct, for instance, and the market can be very different when the project is finished than when it began. Add the possibility of leverage, and risks get even bigger. Insurance is another relevant example. The cost of goods, especially for multiyear policies, is unknown at the time pricing is set.

Risk versus Risk Perception

Risk is not always straightforward. The riskiness of an investment can be strongly affected merely by how risky people perceive it to be. Prior to 2008, residential mortgage loans were viewed as being very low risk—default rates were, in fact, historically low leading up to the crisis. This perception of low risk led to more and more aggressive underwriting and unusual packaging of the cash flows from mortgage-backed securities. The underwriting became worse and worse because people believed that the underlying investments were so low risk, and they desperately wanted to move product into the marketplace, sliced and diced in all sorts of ways.

An investment perceived as low risk became high risk before the perception was able to catch up to the reality, which is how the entire industry ended up crashing. What compounded the problem was that few people actually understood the investments that they were buying. Thus, when problems started to arise, these securities fell dramatically in price. Lehman and AIG tried desperately to unload them since they were deep into these investments, but no one understood the securities well enough to buy them, and prices dropped even further than they perhaps deserved to. Once people started to figure the value out, the price, in fact, had a bit of a comeback. A greater number of people who understand a particular security reduces the risk of dramatic collapse. Here, not enough people knew. Once there was any doubt about the underlying value of the securities, the price fell dramatically. Risk perception reversed, and people ended up assuming they were even riskier than they actually were.

The issue of how understandable an investment is can be very important in evaluating risk versus risk perception. A Treasury bond, for instance, is very easy to understand, with a defined interest rate. If you need to sell it, the market knows what you are selling and can price it accordingly. But if I create a complicated security, and there are only three of us in the world who really understand how to price it, and if all three of us need money at the same time and are trying to sell it, who is going to buy it? The only people who will come forward to purchase will do so at a steep discount because they perceive the risk to be higher than it might actually be simply because they don't understand it. They need to buy at a low price in order to protect themselves against the possibility they have it wrong.

Economic trends that have been going on for a long time also tend to lead to low-risk perceptions that may not turn into reality. People become lazy over time and assume that a long-term economic trend will continue forever. If you've gone a long time without something blowing up, that in itself creates risk because people start doing crazier and crazier things, leading to a degradation in the quality of the investment. The residential real estate crisis was created largely by the assumption that default rates on residential mortgages would always be low. Historically—for decades—default rates on residential mortgages had been low. Assuming this would continue indefinitely, lenders began loaning more and more money to home buyers, requiring lower and lower down payments and doing extreme cash-out refinancing, in some cases lending over 100 percent of the equity value of the home. This led to a very unstable situation where many homeowners could not actually afford the homes they lived in—so default rates rose, and the crisis unfolded.

Similarly, since 1981, interest rates in the US have been in a long and steady decline. Government policy over decades resulted in extremely low rates and the rapid expansion of the money supply. The assumption was that rates would stay low forever—but we have seen recent inflation, followed by a determination on the part of the Federal Reserve Board to raise interest rates in order to reduce it. As of this writing, interest rates are up considerably from their lows. They may need to move even higher. Even at the current level, there are risks to the economy that may not have made themselves known yet since so much investment has been predicated on these "permanently" low rates. People have built into their economic activity the presumption that rates will always be low, and I believe we will face a reckoning as we see the fallout.

As one example: The incredible private equity returns over the past generation have been largely a result of falling interest rates, and investments in those private equity firms are likely to suffer going forward. When private equity takes over a company, they frequently add considerable leverage with short-term debt, then cut expenses, make the company more productive, get a credit upgrade, refinance the debt at a lower rate, and finally take the company public at a higher valuation than they bought it for. But this sequence of events is predicated largely on low (and falling) interest rates. Lower rates create higher valuations, so this has served as a tailwind for private equity for decades. Every time PE firms go to refinance, basic rates tend to be lower. Now, with higher rates and lower valuations, they will not be able to take companies public at the same kinds of higher valuations they've been experiencing—and the industry will see consequences.

Another example: US government debt. Much of the country's debt is fairly short term in terms of aggregate duration, so over the next few years, a lot of that will need to be refinanced, and it's more than 100 percent of GDP now. We think of government debt as low risk, but this is only the case in an environment where interest rates are low. If we are currently financing the debt at an average rate of 2 percent, and the rate suddenly jumps to 5 percent, that's 3 percent of GDP spending on additional interest alone. It's going to put enormous pressure on government spending, combined with the aging population adding concerns to Medicare and Social Security costs. The risk should be obvious—it's not a secret—but no one wants to acknowledge it. The Congressional Budget Office estimates that by 2053, a full 7.2 percent of our GDP will be spent merely on interest servicing the debt.[4]

The end result of this entire discussion: we have so many fancy quantitative tools to measure and assess risk, but we are still left with the fact that real and foreseeable risks are often ignored by the market, and they are vitally important to consider in combination with everything else presented in this book.

CONCLUSION

When I retired as chairman and chief investment officer of Dodge & Cox in 2022, I realized that nearly forty years in this business had taught me so many lessons about investing, but also that many of those lessons were timeless. Whether I was a young investment analyst studying opportunities for the firm or the leader of a team of experienced investors managing hundreds of billions of dollars for families and institutions around the world, many of the principles were very much the same, and I hope this book has given you some insight into the kind of thinking that was required.

I hope these pages have provided you with some concrete ideas to take into account when looking to invest for the long term. In the conclusion, I wanted to offer a summary pulled from each of the chapters—some principles you can carry with you as you put these ideas into practice and bring them to bear in your investing work.

ACCOUNTING

1. Pay attention to when earnings are recognized.
2. If earnings look too smooth, ensure there is nothing

in the background that is engineering them to appear that way.

3. Ensure that the company's reserves are sensible and appropriate.

4. Trust the auditors, but not too much.

5. Use the available models to help ensure the numbers aren't being fudged.

FRANCHISE

1. Think about the concentration of competitors, labor, and customers.

2. Consider the value of patents and copyrights.

3. Give thought to the barriers to entry and the barriers to exit for other companies in the space.

4. Do not underestimate the potential of regulation or changing technologies to alter a company's potential.

5. Be especially mindful of new opportunities in emerging markets.

GOVERNANCE

1. Be wary of overly conscientious or extraverted CEOs, who may not have the aggressive posture necessary to lead well.

2. Look for evidence of a system underlying corporate decision-making and rigorous analysis being

undertaken when it comes to capital allocation.

3. Understand the executive compensation packages and how they align (or misalign) incentives.

4. Note the board composition and the motivations of the board members.

5. Pay attention to differences between domestic and foreign norms when it comes to disclosure and management.

VALUATION

1. Consider the harder-to-value attributes in the company's industry, and try to spend time valuing them.

2. Do not rely too heavily on ratios that may not reflect the business environment today.

FORECASTING

1. Be aware of the behavioral biases that affect us all.

2. Look at the base rates for the industry you are examining, and make sure there are legitimate reasons why a particular company may over- or underperform.

3. Consider all sources of information, not just the most obvious ones.

SELL DISCIPLINE

1. Do not let the desire to prove right the decision to buy keep you from selling.
2. Be as rigorous in examining when to sell as you were in making the initial choice to purchase.

RISK

1. Remember that the past is not always a reliable predictor of the future.
2. Keep in mind the risk of a permanent loss of capital, beyond just the natural ups and downs of the market.
3. Focus on long-term risk even when short-term risk seems low.

Above all, realize that the world is always changing, and the methods that worked for you at one point may not always work in the future. As a tool to keep yourself objective, you may want to keep a log that records your investment thinking for companies you are looking at, including the date you record your observations, thoughts, assumptions, and logic. Update your log regularly, and look back to see whether there has been a drift in your thinking. You need to be able to test your hypotheses over time, which can only happen if you track your expectations. I hope this book has given you plenty to think about, and I wish you luck as you make your investment decisions.

NOTES

CHAPTER 2: ACCOUNTING

1   Baruch Lev and Feng Gu, *The End of Accounting and the Path Forward for Investors and Managers* (Hoboken, NJ: Wiley, 2016).

2   Ibid.

3   Ibid.

4   Howard M. Schilit, Jeremy Perler, and Yoni Engelhart, *Financial Shenanigans, Fourth Edition: How to Detect Accounting Gimmicks and Fraud in Financial Reports* (New York: McGraw-Hill Education, 2018).

5   "MicroStrategy's Curious Success," *Forbes*, March 6, 2000, http://www.forbes.com/global/2000/0306/0305024a.html.

6   Schilit, Perler, and Engelhart, *Financial Shenanigans*.

7   Floyd Norris, "MicroStrategy Chairman Accused of Fraud by S.E.C.," *New York Times*, December 15, 2000, https://www.nytimes.com/2000/12/15/business/microstrategy-chairman-accused-of-fraud-by-sec.html.

8   Michael Bellusci, "SEC Objects to MicroStrategy's Accounting Adjustment for Its Bitcoin Holdings," Yahoo Finance, January 21, 2022, https://finance.yahoo.com/news/microstrategy-bitcoin-accounting-adjustment-rejected-213411449.html.

9   Lauren Feiner, "MicroStrategy Chair Michael Saylor Accused of Evading $25 Million in Taxes by DC Attorney General," CNBC, August 31, 2022, https://www.cnbc.com/2022/08/31/microstrategy-chairman-michael-saylor-accused-of-tax-evasion-by-dc-ag.html.

10 Melanie Drever et al., "Sunbeam Corporation: 'Chainsaw Al,' Greed, and Recovery," ed. O. C. Ferrell and Linda Ferrell, Center for Ethical Organizational Cultures at Auburn University, 2015, https://harbert.

auburn.edu/binaries/documents/center-for-ethical-organizational-cultures/cases/sunbeam.pdf.

11   Ibid.

12   Ibid.

13   Michael J. de la Merced, "Ex-Leader of Computer Associates Gets 12-Year Sentence and Fine," *New York Times*, November 3, 2006, https://www.nytimes.com/2006/11/03/technology/03computer.html.

14   "SEC.gov | Litigation Release: Computer Associates International, Inc., Sanjay Kumar and Stephen Richards, and Steven Woghin," SEC, September 22, 2004, https://www.sec.gov/litigation/litreleases/lr-18891.

15   Others have written about this issue. For instance, see Steve Cooper and Dennis Jullens, "Should You Ignore Intangible Amortisation?—AstraZeneca," The Footnotes Analyst, July 8, 2019, https://www.footnotesanalyst.com/should-you-ignore-intangible-amortisation/.

16   Robert M. Bowen and Jane Jollineau Kennedy, "Exxon Mobil Corporation: The Politics of Profit," University of Washington: Michael G. Foster School of Business (July 2008): https://faculty.washington.edu/rbowen/cases/Exxon%20LIFO%20case_7-08.pdf.

17   "Offshore Disaster: Timeline of Offshore Oil Drilling, Spills, and Regulations," Greenpeace, accessed November 21, 2023, https://www.greenpeace.org/usa/wp-content/uploads/legacy/Global/usa/planet3/PDFs/timeline.pdf.

18   Anne Diamond and Robert V. Diamond, "Fraud at Waste Management," in *Professional Ethics for Accountants* (California 9th Edition: Press Books, 2019), https://pressbooks.pub/professionalethicsforaccountants/chapter/chapter-9/.

19   Diamond and Diamond, "Fraud at Waste Management."

20   Kurt Eichenwald, "Waste Management Executives Are Named in S.E.C. Accusation (Published 2002)," *New York Times*, March 27, 2002, https://www.nytimes.com/2002/03/27/business/waste-management-executives-are-named-in-sec-accusation.html.

21   Walter M. Cadette, "How Stock Options Lead to Scandal," *New York Times*, July 12, 2002, https://www.nytimes.com/2002/07/12/opinion/how-stock-options-lead-to-scandal.html.

22   Schilit, Perler, and Engelhart, *Financial Shenanigans*.

23   Theron Mohamed, "Warren Buffett Blasted Earnings Manipulation as 'Disgusting' in His Annual Letter. Here's What He Meant, and How GE Legend Jack Welch Ties into It," Markets Insider, February 28, 2023, https://markets.businessinsider.com/news/stocks/warren-buffett-berkshire-hathaway-earnings-manipulation-jack-welch-ge-accounting-2023-2.

24   Floyd Norris, "A Satellite Empire: Marketplace; the Tracking Stock Idea Goes into Retirement at G.M.," *New York Times*, April 10, 2003, https://www.nytimes.com/2003/04/10/business/satellite-empire-market-place-tracking-stock-idea-goes-into-retirement-gm.html.

25   Schilit, Perler, and Engelhart, *Financial Shenanigans*.

26   Matt O'Brien, "China's Richest Man Might Have Been Running a Massive Fraud," *Washington Post*, May 27, 2015, https://www.washingtonpost.com/news/wonk/wp/2015/05/27/chinas-richest-man-might-have-been-running-a-massive-fraud/.

27   Ryan General, "Energy Tycoon Li Hejun, Once China's Richest Man, Arrested," Yahoo News, January 13, 2023, https://news.yahoo.com/energy-tycoon-li-hejun-once-180029462.html.

28   Matt Nesvisky, "Pension Assumptions and Earnings Manipulation," National Bureau of Economic Research, December 2004, https://www.nber.org/digest/dec04/pension-assumptions-and-earnings-manipulation.

29   Ibid.

30   Schilit, Perler, and Engelhart, *Financial Shenanigans*.

31   Peter E. Greulich, "IBM's First Attempt at Financial Engineering Ended in Near Disaster," Discerning Readers, August 9, 2021, https://www.discerningreaders.com/ibm-john-opel-first-attempt-financial-engineering.html.

32   Schilit, Perler, and Engelhart, *Financial Shenanigans*.

33   "Cendant Corporation," SEC, June 14, 2000, https://www.sec.gov/litigation/admin/34-42933.

34   "Asbestos Litigation: KCIC Industry Report: 2022 Year in Review," KCIC, 2023, https://www.kcic.com/media/2253/kcic_asbestos2022report.pdf.

35 Michelle J. White, "Explaining the Flood of Asbestos Litigation: Consolidation, Bifurcation, and Bouquet Trials" (working paper, National Bureau of Economic Research, December 2002), http://www.nber.org/papers/w9362.

36 John Flesher, "3M Reaches $10.3 Billion Settlement over Contamination of Water Systems with 'Forever Chemicals,'" AP News, June 23, 2023, https://apnews.com/article/pfas-forever-chemicals-3m-drinking-water-81775af23d6aeae63533796b1a1d2cdb.

37 Byron J. McLain and Cole K. Waldhauser, "Carbon Neutrality Suit against Delta Airlines Signals the Arrival Time of 'Greenwashing' Litigation," Foley & Lardner LLP, June 15, 2023, https://www.foley.com/insights/publications/2023/06/carbon-neutrality-suit-delta-airlines-greenwashing/.

38 "Our Net-Zero Journey," Holcim, https://www.holcim.com/sustainability/climate-action/our-net-zero-journey, accessed March 27, 2024.

39 "SEC Charges Satyam Computer Services with Financial Fraud," SEC, April 5, 2011, https://www.sec.gov/news/press/2011/2011-81.htm.

40 Sudhakar (Sid) V. Balachandran, "The Satyam Scandal," *Forbes*, January 7, 2009, https://www.forbes.com/2009/01/07/satyam-raju-governance-oped-cx_sb_0107balachandran.html?sh=68b13a903044.

41 Erica Shaffer, "SEC, Utah Firm Settle Case over Chinese Poultry Business," Meat+Poultry, February 3, 2015, https://www.meatpoultry.com/articles/12459-sec-utah-firm-settle-case-over-chinese-poultry-business.

42 Peter Molk and Frank Partnoy, "The Long-Term Effects of Short Selling and Negative Activism the Long-Term Effects of Short Selling and Negative Activism," 2022, https://scholarship.law.ufl.edu/cgi/viewcontent.cgi?article=2099&context=facultypub.

43 Elliot Smith, "The Barings Collapse 25 Years On: What the Industry Learned after One Man Broke a Bank," CNBC, February 26, 2020, https://www.cnbc.com/2020/02/26/barings-collapse-25-years-on-what-the-industry-learned-after-one-man-broke-a-bank.html.

44 Andrew Beattie, "How Did Nick Leeson Contribute to the Fall of Barings Bank?," Investopedia, March 23, 2020, https://www.investopedia.com/ask/answers/08/nick-leeson-barings-bank.asp.

45 Elliot Smith, "The Barings Collapse 25 Years On: What the Industry Learned after One Man Broke a Bank," CNBC, February 26, 2020,

https://www.cnbc.com/2020/02/26/barings-collapse-25-years-on-what-the-industry-learned-after-one-man-broke-a-bank.html.

46   "Rogue Trader Nick Leeson Who Brought down a Bank Turns Investigator of Financial Misdeeds," *The Straits Times*, March 22, 2023, https://www.straitstimes.com/business/former-british-rogue-trader-who-served-time-in-s-pore-prison-reemerges-as-a-private-spy.

47   I. J. Alexander Dyck, Adair Morse, and Luigi Zingales, "How Pervasive Is Corporate Fraud?" (working paper, University of Toronto: Rotman School of Management Research Paper Series, Rotman School of Management, February 18, 2021), http://dx.doi.org/10.2139/ssrn.2222608.

48   Schilit, Perler, and Engelhart, *Financial Shenanigans*.

49   Rimkus, "Parmalat," Financial Scandals, Scoundrels & Crises, November 29, 2016, https://www.econcrises.org/2016/11/29/parmalat/.

50   Schilit, Perler, and Engelhart, *Financial Shenanigans*.

51   Rimkus, "Parmalat."

52   Jim Frost, "Benford's Law Explained with Examples," Statistics By Jim, October 6, 2022, https://statisticsbyjim.com/probability/benfords-law/.

53   Messod D. Beneish, "The Detection of Earnings Manipulation," Financial Analysts Journal 55, no. 5 (September 1999): 24–36.

CHAPTER 3: FRANCHISE

1   Peter Brown, "94% of DRAM Market Controlled by Three Companies," Electronics360, May 25, 2022, https://electronics360.globalspec.com/article/18157/94-of-dram-market-controlled-by-three-companies.

2   Kunio Okina, Masaaki Shirakawa, and Shigenori Shiratsuka, "Financial Market Globalization: Present and Future," *Monetary and Economic Studies* 17, no. 3 (1999) p.1–40, https://www.imes.boj.or.jp/research/papers/english/me17-3-1.pdf. Graph reproduced with permission.

3   Nils Behnke, Michael Retterath, Todd Sangster and Ashish Singh, "New Paths to Value Creation in Pharma," Bain and Company, September 24, 2014, https://www.bain.com/insights/new-paths-to-value-creation-in-pharma/. Figure used with permission from Bain and Company.

4   Rob Copeland and Maureen Farrell, "First Republic Lurches as It Struggles to Find a Savior," *New York Times*, April 26, 2023, https://www.nytimes.com/2023/04/26/business/first-republic-bank.html.

5   Dave Farquhar, "286 vs. 386SX," The Silicon Underground, August 18, 2021, https://dfarq.homeip.net/286-vs-386sx/.

6   "1989–Paving the Way to a 32-Bit World," Intel, 1989, https://www.intel.com/content/www/us/en/history/history-1989-annual-report.html. Figure used with permission.

7   Chris Aspin and Cyntia Barrera Diaz, "Mexico's Telmex Says Spin-off Rumor False," Reuters, August 9, 2007, https://www.reuters.com/article/idUSN08347028/.

8   Greg Iacurci, "GE Expects $1.7 Billion in Rate Increases for Long-Term Care Policies," InvestmentNews, March 7, 2019, https://www.investmentnews.com/industry-news/features/ge-expects-1-7-billion-in-rateincreases-for-long-term-care-policies-78491.

9   Matt Scuffham, "Exclusive: Deutsche Bank's Problem Derivatives Cloud Recovery - Sources," Reuters, July 23, 2019, https://www.reuters.com/article/idUSKCN1UI2TR/.

10 "Apple Worth More than the Entire Russell 2000, Will the Trend Continue?," Business Insider, May 16, 2023, https://markets.businessinsider. com/news/etf/apple-worth-more-than-the-entire-russell-2000-willthe-trend-continue-1032331041.

11 Jay Shambaugh, Ryan Nunn, and Becca Portman, "Eleven Facts about Innovation and Patents," The Hamilton Project, December 13, 2017, https://www.hamiltonproject.org/publication/economic-fact/eleven-facts-about-innovation-and-patents.

12 US Census Bureau, "Census Bureau Releases New Educational Attainment Data," Census.gov, 2022, https://www.census.gov/newsroom/press-releases/2022/educational-attainment.html.

13 Daniel Kaufmann, Homi Kharas, and Veronika Penciakova, "Development, Aid, and Governance Indicators (DAGI)," Brookings, July 18, 2012, https://www.brookings.edu/articles/development-aid-and-governance-indicators-dagi/. Figure used with permission14

14 Figure used with permission of Bloomberg.

CHAPTER 4: GOVERNANCE

1   Steven Kaplan, Mark M. Klebanov, and Morten Sorensen, "NBER Working Paper Series: Which CEO Characteristics And Abilities Mat-

ter?," 2008, https://www.nber.org/system/files/working_papers/w14195/w14195.pdf.

2   Kaplan, Klebanov, and Sorensen, "Which CEO Characteristics And Abilities Matter?"

3   Ian D. Gow, Steven N. Kaplan, David F. Larcker, and Anastasia A. Zakolyukina, "CEO Personality and Firm Policies," *SSRN Electronic Journal* (2016): https://doi.org/10.2139/ssrn.2805635.

4   Geoff Smart and Randy Street, *Who* (New York: Ballantine Books, 2008).

5   Ibid.

6   Brian O'Connell, "The Damage Done: Dealing with Narcissists in the Workplace," SHRM, February 23, 2021, https://www.shrm.org/resource-sandtools/hr-topics/people-managers/pages/narcissism-and-manag-ers-.aspx.

7   James W. Pennebaker, *The Secret Life of Pronouns: What Our Words Say about Us* (New York: Bloomsbury Press, 2013).

8   Tae Kim, "Warren Buffett on Judging Management: 'See How They Treat Themselves versus How They Treat the Shareholders,'" CNBC, May 9, 2018, https://www.cnbc.com/2018/05/08/warren-buffett-heres-how-to-judge-management.html.

9   Richard Guzman, "Barry Minkow Got Famous Cheating the System—Now He's Back with 'King of the Con,'" *Daily News*, January 11, 2022, https://www.dailynews.com/2022/01/11/barry-minkow-got-famous-cheating-the-system-now-hes-back-with-king-of-the-con/.

10 Rebecca Stuart, "Why Did Credit Suisse Fail and What Does It Mean for Banking Regulation?," Economics Observatory, April 13, 2023, https://www.economicsobservatory.com/why-did-credit-suisse-fail-and-what-does-it-mean-for-banking-regulation.

11 Allen R. Myerson, "Raytheon Wins Arms Unit in Texas, Though at High Price," *New York Times*, January 7, 1997, https://www.nytimes.com/1997/01/07/business/raytheon-wins-arms-unit-in-texas-though-at-high-price.html.

12 "TI to Sell DRAM Business to Micron," *EE Times*, June 18, 1998, https://www.eetimes.com/ti-to-sell-dram-business-to-micron/.

13 Sami Lais, "VeriSign Restructuring Close to Finish Line," *Washington Technology*, October 29, 2009, https://washingtontechnology.com/2009/10/verisign-restructuring-close-to-finish-line/323252/.

14 Stefanie Hoffman, "Symantec to Acquire VeriSign Security for $1.28B," CRN, May 19, 2010, https://www.crn.com/news/security/224900438/symantec-to-acquire-verisign-security-for-1-28b.htm.

15 Jon Oltsik, "The Other Side of the Symantec/Verisign Deal," CSO, May 21, 2010, https://www.csoonline.com/article/2230802/the-other-side-of-the-symantec-verisign-deal.html.

16 "Danaher Business System," Danaher, 2020, https://www.danaher.com/how-we-work/danaher-business-system.

17 Daniela Scur, Raffaella Sadun, John Van Reenen, Renata Lemos, and Nicholas Bloom, "World Management Survey at 18: Lessons and the Way Forward," *SSRN Electronic Journal* (2021): https://doi.org/10.2139/ssrn.3794092.

18 Nicholas Bloom, Renata Lemos, Raffaella Sadun, Daniela Scur, and John Van Reenen "The New Empirical Economics of Management," *Journal of the European Economic Association* 12, no. 4 (July 15, 2014): 835–76, https://doi.org/10.1111/jeea.12094.

19 John E. Doerr, *Measure What Matters: How Google, Bono, and the Gates Foundation Rock the World with OKRs* (New York: Portfolio, 2018).

20 Michael Roberts, "Making Sense of Stock Buybacks," *Knowledge at Wharton*, March 7, 2023, https://knowledge.wharton.upenn.edu/article/making-sense-of-stock-buybacks/.

21 Robert F. Bruner, *Deals from Hell: M&A Lessons That Rise above the Ashes* (Hoboken, NJ: Wiley, 2005).

22 "Timeline | History of Union Pacific," Union Pacific, https://www.up.com/timeline/index.cfm, accessed March 27, 2024.

23 Don Phillips, "Union Pacific to Merge with Southern Pacific," August 4, 1995, http://washingtonpost.com/archive/business/1995/08/04/union-pacific-to-merge-with-southern-pacific/8eded38e-d307-4c2f-8738-bce411d10e43/.

24 Brian O'Reilly, "The Wreck of the Union Pacific: In Its Glory Days, UP Completed the Transcontinental Railroad. It Always Had the Best Locomotives and the Best Track. But It Derailed When It Acquired

Southern Pacific," CNN Money, March 30, 1998, https://money.cnn.com/magazines/fortune/fortune_archive/1998/03/30/240141/index.htm.

25 Daniel Machalaba, "Problems in Wake of Merger Continue for Union Pacific," *Wall Street Journal*, October 2, 1997, https://www.wsj.com/articles/SB875724698120686000.

26 Denis A. Breen, "The Union Pacific/Southern Pacific Rail Merger: A Retrospective on Merger Benefits," *SSRN Electronic Journal* (2004): https://doi.org/10.2139/ssrn.531222.

27 Alfred Rappaport and Mark Sirower, "Stock or Cash?: The Trade-Offs for Buyers and Sellers in Mergers and Acquisitions," *Harvard Business Review*, August 2014, https://hbr.org/1999/11/stock-or-cash-the-trade-offs-for-buyers-and-sellers-in-mergers-and-acquisitions.

28 Shane Shifflett, "Executive Stock Sales Are under Scrutiny. Here's What Regulators Are Interested In," *Wall Street Journal*, August 11, 2021, https://www.wsj.com/articles/executive-stock-sales-are-under-scrutiny-heres-what-regulators-are-interested-in-11628682985.

29 David Larcker, Bradford Lynch, Phillip Quinn, Brian Tayan, and Daniel J. Taylor "Gaming the System: Three 'Red Flags' of Potential 10B5-1 Abuse," Stanford Closer Look Series, January 19, 2021, https://www.gsb.stanford.edu/sites/default/files/publication-pdf/cgri-closer-look-88-gaming-the-system.pdf.

30 Anthony Moore, "Want to Be Insanely Successful? Put All Your Eggs in One Basket," Thrive Global, May 23, 2019, https://thriveglobal.com/stories/want-to-be-insanely-successful-put-all-your-eggs-in-one-basket/.

31 Phoebe Mogharei, "From the Vault: Spoiled Fruit," *Chicago Magazine*, October 4, 2018, https://www.chicagomag.com/chicago-magazine/october-2018/from-the-vault-spoiled-fruit/.

32 Ibid.

33 Michael C. Jensen and Jerold L. Zimmerman, "Management Compensation and the Managerial Labor Market," *Journal of Accounting and Economics* 7, no. 1–3 (April 1985): 3–9, https://doi.org/10.1016/0165-4101(85)90025-.4.

34 Kevin J. Murphy, "Executive Compensation," *SSRN Electronic Journal* (April 1998): https://ssrn.com/abstract=163914.

35 Kevin J. Murphy and Michael C. Jensen, "CEO Bonus Plans: And How to Fix Them," SSRN Electronic Journal (November 19, 2011): https://ssrn.com/abstract=1935654.

36 David Larcker and Brian Tayan, *Corporate Governance Matters* (FT Press, 2011).

37 Alex Edmans, Xavier Gabaix, and Dirk Jenter, "Executive Compensation: A Survey of Theory and Evidence," *The Handbook of the Economics of Corporate Governance*, 2017, 383–539, https://doi.org/10.1016/bs.hecg.2017.11.010. Reprinted with permission.

38 Marco Becht, Patrick Bolton, and Alisa A. Röell, "Corporate Governance and Control," *SSRN Electronic Journal* (October 2002): https://ssrn.com/abstract=343461.

39 Patrick Seitz, "Microchip Stock Drops on Word It Inherits Mess from Microsemi Deal," *Investor's Business Daily*, August 10, 2018, https://www.investors.com/news/technology/microchip-stock-microsemi-inventory/.

40 Bill Gurley, X (blog), January 4, 2023, https://x.com/bgurley/status/1610794652243996672?s=20.

41 David Yermack, "Higher Market Valuation of Companies with a Small Board of Directors," *Journal of Financial Economics* 40, no. 2 (February 1996): 185–211.

42 Y. T. Mak and Yuanto Kusnadi, "Size Really Matters: Further Evidence on the Negative Relationship between Board Size and Firm Value," *Pacific-Basin Finance Journal* 13, no. 3 (June 2005): 301–18, https://doi.org/10.1016/j.pacfin.2004.09.002.

43 Sanjai Bhagat and Bernard S. Black, "The Non-Correlation between Board Independence and Long-Term Firm Performance" (working paper, Stanford Law and Economics Olin, October 3, 1998), https://ssrn.com/abstract=13380.4

44 Rüdiger Fahlenbrach, Angie Low, and Rene M. Stulz, "Why Do Firms Appoint CEOs as Outside Directors?" (working paper, Fisher College of Business, Charles A. Dice Center for Research in Financial Economics, July 2008), https://ssrn.com/abstract=116027.

45 A. Burak Güner, Ulrike Malmendier, and Geoffrey Tate, "Financial Expertise of Directors," Journal of Financial Economics 88, no. 2 (May 2008): 323–54, https://doi.org/10.1016/j.jfineco.2007.05.009.

46 Ibid.

47 Anup Agrawal and Charles R. Knoeber, "Firm Performance and Mechanisms to Control Agency Problems between Managers and Shareholders," *The Journal of Financial and Quantitative Analysis* 31, no. 3 (September 1996): 377–97, https://doi.org/10.2307/2331487.

48 Larcker and Tayan, *Corporate Governance Matters*.

49 Francois Dauphin and Yvan Allaire, "A 'Successful' Case of Activism at the Canadian Pacific Railway: Lessons in Corporate Governance," The Harvard Law School Forum on Corporate Governance, December 23, 2016, https://corpgov.law.harvard.edu/2016/12/23/a-successful-case-of-activism-at-the-canadian-pacific-railway-lessons-in-corporate-governance/.

50 Ibid.

51 Jacquie McNish, "William Ackman Takes Stake in Canadian Pacific," *Wall Street Journal*, March 7, 2022, https://www.wsj.com/articles/activist-william-ackman-takes-stake-in-canadian-pacific-11646671278.

52 James J. Cordeiro, Rajaram Veliyath, and Donald O. Neubaum, "Incentives for Monitors: Director Stock-Based Compensation and Firm Performance," *Journal of Applied Business Research* 21, no. 2 (January 18, 2011): https://doi.org/10.19030/jabr.v21i2.1491.

53 Ivan E. Brick, Oded Palmon, and John K. Wald, "CEO Compensation, Director Compensation, and Firm Performance: Evidence of Cronyism?," *Journal of Corporate Finance* 12, no. 3 (June 2006): 403–23, https://doi.org/10.1016/j.jcorpfin.2005.08.00.

54 Adam C. Pritchard, Stephen P. Ferris, and Murali Jagannathan, "Too Busy to Mind the Business? Monitoring by Directors with Multiple Board Appointments, *SSRN Electronic Journal* (June 2002): https://ssrn.com/abstract=167288.

55 Eliezer M. Fich and Anil Shivdasani, "Are Busy Boards Effective Monitors?," *The Journal of Finance* 61, no. 2 (March 9, 2006): 689–724, https://doi.org/10.1111/j.1540-6261.2006.00852.x.

56 Randall K. Morck, *A History of Corporate Governance around the World* (University of Chicago Press, 2007). Chart used with permission.

57 David Mullins, "Does the Capital Asset Pricing Model Work?," *Harvard Business Review*, January 1982, https://hbr.org/1982/01/does-the-capital-asset-pricing-model-work.

58 Larcker and Tayan, *Corporate Governance Matters.*

59 Belen Villalonga and Raphael Amit, "How Do Family Ownership, Control, and Management Affect Firm Value?," *Journal of Financial Economics* 80, no. 2 (May 2006): 385–417, https://doi.org/10.1016/j.jfineco.2004.12.005.

60 Moysich and Alane, "The Savings and Loan Crisis and Its Relationship and Its Relationship to Banking to Banking," 1998, https://www.fdic.gov/bank/historical/history/167_188.pdf.

61 "McKinsey & Company Investor Opinion Survey," June 2000, https://www.oecd.org/daf/ca/corporategovernanceprinciples/1922101.pdf.

62 Art Durnev and E. Han Kim, "To Steal or Not to Steal: Firm Attributes, Legal Environment, and Valuation," *Journal of Finance* 60, no. 3 (May 3, 2005): 1461–93, https://doi.org/10.1111/j.1540-6261.2005.00767.x.

63 Daniela Scur, Raffaella Sadun, John Van Reenen, Renata Lemos, and Nicholas Bloom, "World Management Survey at 18: Lessons and the Way Forward," *SSRN Electronic Journal* (2021): https://doi.org/10.2139/ssrn.3794092.

64 See: Larcker and Tayan, *Corporate Governance Matters*; Morck, *A History of Corporate Governance around the World* (University of Chicago Press, 2007); Thomas Clarke, *International Corporate Governance* (Routledge, 2023); Christine Mallin, *Handbook on International Corporate Governance: Country Analyses* (Cheltenham, UK: Edward Elgar Publishing, 2011).

65 Charles C. Kenney, *Riding the Runaway Horse: The Rise and Decline of Wang Laboratories* (New York: Little, Brown and Company, 1992).

CHAPTER 5: VALUATION

1 James P. O'Shaughnessy, *What Works on Wall Street: The Classic Guide to the Best-Performing Investment Strategies of All Time* (New York: McGraw Hill, 2012).

2 Ki-Soon Choi, Eric C. So, and Charles C. Y. Wang, "Going by the Book: Valuation Ratios and Stock Returns," *SSRN Electronic Journal* (2021): https://doi.org/10.2139/ssrn.3854022.

3 Darío Gil, "Why IBM Is No Longer Interested in Breaking Patent Records—and How It Plans to Measure Innovation in the Age of Open Source and Quantum Computing," *Fortune*, January 6, 2023, https://

fortune.com/2023/01/06/ibm-patent-record-how-to-measure-innova-tion-open-source-quantum-computing-tech/.

4   Adi Robertson, "AOL Sells Majority of Patent Portfolio to Microsoft in Billion-Dollar Deal," The Verge, April 9, 2012, https://www.theverge.com/2012/4/9/2935624/aol-sells-800-patents-to-microsoft-1-billion-li-censing-deal.

CHAPTER 6: FORECASTING

1   Philip Tetlock and Dan Gardner, *Superforecasting* (New York: Random House, 2015).

2   Paul Saffo, "Strong Opinions Weakly Held," Paul Saffo, July 26, 2008, https://saffo.com/02008/07/26/strong-opinions-weakly-held/.

3   Robert J. Shiller, "Human Behavior and the Efficiency of the Financial System," www.econ.yale.edu, September 27, 1997, http://www.econ.yale.edu/~shiller/online/handbook.html.

4   Ibid.

5   Ibid.

6   Ibid.

7   Ibid.

8   Andrew Shilling, "George Soros Has a Big Stake in This Stock—but It's Posted a Roughly 8.5% Loss This Year. Are There Lessons in This for Regular Investors?," MarketWatch, August 17, 2023, https://www.marketwatch.com/picks/george-soros-has-a-big-stake-in-this-stock-but-its-posted-a-roughly-9-loss-this-year-are-there-lessons-in-this-for-regular-investors-182afad0#.

9   Glassdoor, "Glassdoor Job Search," December 31, 2007, https://www.glassdoor.com.

10 E. Scott Reckard, "Wells Fargo Accuses Workers of Opening Fake Accounts to Meet Goals," *Los Angeles Times*, October 3, 2013, https://www.latimes.com/business/la-xpm-2013-oct-03-la-fi-1004-wells-fargo-firings-20131004-story.html.

11 Paul Kunert, "Former DXC Technology Veep Accuses 'Toxic' CEO Lawrie of Bullying Staff in Lawsuit," The Register, February 12, 2019, https://www.theregister.com/2019/02/12/dxc_technology_former_veep_accuses_toxic_ceo_lawrie_of_bullying/.

12 Ibid.

13 T. Clifton Green, Ruoyan Huang, Quan Wen, and Dexin Zhou, "Crowd-sourced Employer Reviews and Stock Returns" (working paper, *Journal of Financial Economics*, 8th Miami Behavioral Finance Conference 2017, April 1, 2018), https://ssrn.com/abstract=3002707.

14 Johnny Hopkins, "Michael Mauboussin: The Importance of Utilizing Base Rates | the Acquirer's Multiple®," The Acquirer's Multiple, January 28, 2021, https://acquirersmultiple.com/2021/01/michael-mauboussin-the-importance-of-utilizing-base-rates/.

15 "Case Studies in Business and Management—IBS CDC," IBS Center for Management Research, 2004, http://www.ibscdc.org/Case_Studies/Marketing/Marketing/LVMH-Marketing%20Case%20Study.htm.

CHAPTER 7: SELL DISCIPLINE

1 Klakow Akepanidtaworn, Rick Di Mascio, Alex Imas, and Lawrence Schmidt, "Selling Fast and Buying Slow: Heuristics and Trading Performance of Institutional Investors," National Bureau of Economic Research, July 1, 2021, https://doi.org/10.3386/w29076.

CHAPTER 8: RISK

1 Robert A. Weigand, "The recovery of US commercial banking: an analysis of revenues, profits, dividends, capital, and value creation," *Banks and Bank Systems* 8, no. 3 (2013). Image courtesy of Robert A. Weigand.

2 True Tamplin, "Mean Reversion," Finance Strategists, July 19, 2023, https://www.financestrategists.com/wealth-management/fundamental-vs-technical-analysis/mean-reversion/.

3 Coryanne Hicks, "Different Types of Cryptocurrencies – Forbes Advisor," www.forbes.com, March 15, 2023, https://www.forbes.com/advisor/investing/cryptocurrency/different-types-of-cryptocurrencies.

4 Congressional Budget Office, "An Update to the Budget Outlook: 2023 to 2033, May 2023; and Office of Management and Budget, Historical Tables, Budget of the United States Government, Fiscal Year 2024," March 2023, used by the Peter G. Peterson Foundation in "Selected Charts on the Long-Term Fiscal Challenges of the United States," December 2023, https://www.pgpf.org/sites/default/files/PGPF-Chart-Pack.pdf.

ACKNOWLEDGMENTS

I learned a great deal of my investment knowledge from John Gunn. Also contributing to my investment knowledge were Dan Rie, Bill Fouse, Bill Sharpe, and David Hoeft. In school, I was taught by Myron Scholes, George Stigler, Jim Lorie, Richard Leftwich, and Doug Diamond. It is notable that three of them won Nobel Prizes, as did Bill Sharpe. Clearly, I had a great education. Helpful comments on the manuscript were provided by David Hoeft, Roberta Kameda, Roger Kuo, Robert Turley, and Jose Ursua. Any errors are my own.

I could not have written this book without a great deal of help from Jeremy Blachman.

ABOUT THE AUTHOR

Charles F. Pohl is the former chairman and chief investment officer at Dodge & Cox, the mutual fund management company with the greatest performance record among its peers over any long-term period. In 2014, he received (along with Director of International Equity Diana Strandberg) the Morningstar Award for International-Stock Fund Manager of the Year. He holds a bachelor's degree and an MBA from the University of Chicago. He lives in San Francisco.